THE BIG BOOK OF
INSTANT POT
RECIPES

Make Healthy and Delicious Breakfasts, Dinners, Soups, and Desserts

HOPE COMERFORD, DAVID MURPHY,
AND BRYAN WOOLLEY

Good Books

New York, New York

Good Books books may be purchased in bulk at special discounts for sales promotion, corporate gifts, fund-raising, or educational purposes. Special editions can also be created to specifications. For details, contact the Special Sales Department, Good Books, 307 West 36th Street, 11th Floor, New York, NY 10018 or info@skyhorsepublishing.com.

Good Books in an imprint of Skyhorse Publishing, Inc.®, a Delaware corporation.

Visit our website at www.goodbooks.com.

10 9 8 7 6 5 4 3 2 1

Library of Congress Cataloging-in-Publication Data is available on file.

The recipes in this book originally appeared in *Fix-It and Forget-It Instant Pot Cookbook* by Hope Comerford, *Fix-It and Forget-It Instant Pot Diabetes Cookbook* by Hope Comerford, *Instant Pot Magic* by David Murphy, and *The Everyday Instant Pot Cookbook* by Bryan Woolley.

Cover design by Daniel Brount
Cover photo credit: Meredith Special Interest Media

Print ISBN: 978-1-68099-561-9
Ebook ISBN: 978-1-68099-562-6

Printed in China

Table of Contents

Welcome to the Instant Pot!

An Instant Pot is a digital pressure cooker that has various other functions. Depending on the model of Instant Pot you have, you can also use other functions besides pressure cooking like sauté, cook rice, multigrains, porridge, soup/stew, beans/chili, meat, poultry, cake, eggs, yogurt, steam, or slow cook—and you can even set it manually. Because the Instant Pot has so many functions, you will no longer need to squeeze multiple appliances on your kitchen counter or use different pots and pans.

Getting Started with the Water Test

The first thing most Instant Pot owners do is called the water test, which helps you to familiarize yourself with the Instant Pot.

Step 1: Plug in your Instant Pot.

Step 2: Make sure the inner pot is inserted in the cooker. You should *never* attempt to cook anything in your device without the inner pot, or you will ruin your Instant Pot. Food should never come into contact with the actual housing unit.

Step 3: The inner pot has lines for each cup. Fill the inner pot with water until it reaches the 3-cup line.

Step 4: Check the sealing ring to make sure it's secure and in place. You should not be able to move it around. If it's not in place properly, you may experience issues with the pot letting out a lot of steam while cooking, or not coming to pressure.

Step 5: Seal the lid. There is an arrow on the lid between "open" and "close." There is also an arrow on the top of the base of the Instant Pot between a picture of a locked lock and an unlocked lock. Line those arrows up, then turn the lid toward the picture of the lock (left). You will hear a noise that will indicate that the lid is locked. If you do not hear a noise, it's not locked.

Step 6: *Always* check to see if the steam valve on top of the lid is turned to "sealing." If it's not on "sealing" and is on "venting," it will not be able to come to pressure.

Step 7: Press the "Steam" button and use the +/- arrow to set it to 2 minutes. Once it's at the desired time, you don't need to press anything else. In a few seconds, the Instant Pot will begin on its own. Note: there is no "start" button on the Instant Pot.

Step 8: The "cooking" will begin once the device comes to pressure. This can take anywhere from 5 to 30 minutes. You will see the countdown begin from the time you set it to. The Instant Pot will beep when your meal is done.

Step 9: Your Instant Pot will now automatically switch to "warm" and begin a count of how many minutes it's been on warm. The next part is where you either wait for the NPR, or natural pressure release (meaning the pressure releases all on its own), or you do what's called a QPR, or quick pressure release (meaning you manually release the pressure). Which method you choose depends on what you're cooking, but in this case, you can choose either since it's just water. For NPR, wait for the lever to move all the way back over to "venting" and watch the pinion (float valve) next to the lever. It will be flush with the lid when at full pressure and will drop when the pressure is done releasing. If you choose QPR, be very careful not to have your hands over the vent as the steam is very hot and you can burn yourself.

What the Buttons Do

A majority of recipes will use the following three most important buttons:

Manual/Pressure Cook: The exact name of this button will vary on your model of Instant Pot. Older models may say "Manual" and newer models may say "Pressure Cook." They mean the same thing. From here, use the +/- button to change the cook time. After several seconds, the Instant Pot will begin its process.

Sauté: For some recipes, you will need to sauté vegetables or brown meat before beginning the pressure-cooking process. For this setting, you will not use the lid of the Instant Pot.

Keep Warm/Cancel: If you forget to use the +/- buttons to change the time for a recipe or if you press a wrong button, you can hit "keep warm/cancel" and it will turn your Instant Pot off.

Here are a list of other buttons and what they do:

Soup/Broth: This function cooks at high pressure for 30 minutes. It can be adjusted using the +/- buttons to cook more for 40 or less for 20 minutes.

Meat/Stew: This function cooks food at high pressure for 35 minutes. It can be adjusted using the +/- buttons to cook more for 45 minutes or less for 20 minutes.

Bean/Chili: This function cooks at high pressure for 30 minutes. It can be adjusted using the +/- buttons to cook more for 40 minutes or less for 25 minutes.

Poultry: This function cooks at high pressure for 15 minutes. It can be adjusted using the +/- buttons to cook more for 30 minutes or less for 5 minutes.

Rice: This function cooks at low pressure and is the only fully automatic program. It is for cooking white rice and will automatically adjust the cooking time depending on the amount of water and rice in the cooking pot.

Multigrain: This function cooks at high pressure for 40 minutes. It can be adjusted using the +/- buttons to cook more for 45 minutes of warm water soaking time and 60 minutes pressure cooking time, or less for 20 minutes.

Porridge: This function cooks at high pressure for 20 minutes. It can be adjusted using the +/- buttons to cook more for 30 minutes or less for 15 minutes.

Steam: This function cooks at high pressure for 10 minutes. It can be adjusted using the +/- buttons to cook more for 15 minutes or less for 3 minutes. Always use a rack or steamer basket with this function because it heats at full power continuously while it's coming to pressure—and you do not want food in direct contact with the bottom of the pressure-cooking pot or it will burn. Once it reaches pressure, the steam button regulates pressure by cycling on and off, similar to the other pressure buttons.

Less | Normal | More: Adjust between the "Less," "Normal," and "More" settings by pressing the same cooking function button repeatedly until you get to the desired setting. Older versions use the Adjust button.

+/- Buttons: Adjust the cook time up [+] or down [-]. On newer models, you can also press and hold [-] or [+] for 3 seconds to turn sound off or on.

Cake: This function cooks at high pressure for 30 minutes. It can be adjusted using the +/- buttons to cook more for 40 minutes or less for 25 minutes.

Egg: This function cooks at high pressure for 5 minutes. It can be adjusted using the +/- buttons to cook more for 6 minutes or less for 4 minutes.

Instant Pot Tips and Tricks

- Do not cook directly in the Instant Pot without the inner pot!
- Once you set the time, you can walk away. The Instant Pot will show the time you set it to, then it will change to the word "on" while the pressure builds. Once the Instant Pot has come to pressure, you will once again see the time you set it for. It will count down from there.
- Always make sure your sealing ring is securely in place. If it shows signs of wear or tear, it needs to be replaced.
- Have a sealing ring for savory recipes and a separate sealing ring for sweet recipes. Many people report their desserts tasting like savory food if they try to use the same sealing ring for all recipes.
- The stainless steel rack (trivet) that your Instant Pot comes with can be used to keep food from being completely submerged in liquid, like baked potatoes or ground beef. It can also be used to set another pot on, for pot-in-pot cooking.
- If you use warm or hot liquid instead of cold liquid, you may need to adjust the cooking time or your food may not come out done.
- Always double-check to see that the valve on the lid is set to "sealing" and not "venting" when you first lock the lid. This will save you from your Instant Pot not coming to pressure.
- Use natural pressure release for tougher cuts of meat, recipes with high starch (like rice or grains), and recipes with a high volume of liquid. This means you let the Instant Pot naturally release pressure. The little bobbin will fall once pressure is released completely.
- Use quick release for more delicate cuts of meat and vegetables—like seafood, chicken breasts, and steaming vegetables. This means you manually turn the vent

(being careful not to put your hand over the vent!) to release the pressure. The little bobbin will fall once pressure is released completely.

- Make sure there is a clear pathway for the steam to release. The last thing you want is to ruin the bottom of your cupboards with the steam.
- You *must* use liquid in your Instant Pot. The minimum amount of liquid you should have in your inner pot is ½ cup; however, most recipes work best with at least 1 cup.
- Do *not* overfill your Instant Pot! It should only be half full for rice or beans (food that expands greatly when cooked) or two-thirds full for almost everything else. Do not fill it to the max filled line.
- If your Instant Pot is not coming to pressure, it's usually because the sealing ring is not on properly, or the vent is not set to "sealing."
- The more liquid, or the colder the ingredients, the longer it will take for the Instant Pot to come to pressure.
- Always make sure that the Instant Pot is dry before inserting the inner pot, and make sure the inner pot is dry before inserting it into the Instant Pot.
- Doubling a recipe does not change the cook time, but instead it will take longer to come up to pressure.
- You do not always need to double the liquid when doubling a recipe. Depending on what you're making, more liquid may make your food too watery. Use your best judgment.
- When using the slow cooker function, use the following chart:

Slow Cooker	Instant Pot
Warm	Less or Low
Low	Normal or Medium
High	More or High

Breakfast & Brunch

Hard-Boiled Eggs

Colleen Heatwole

Makes 6–8 servings

1 cup water
6–8 eggs

1. Pour the water into the inner pot. Place the eggs in a steamer basket or rack that came with pot.

2. Close the lid and secure to the locking position. Be sure the vent is turned to sealing. Set for 5 minutes on Manual at high pressure. (It takes about 5 minutes for pressure to build and then 5 minutes to cook.)

3. Let pressure naturally release for 5 minutes, then do quick pressure release.

4. Place hot eggs into cool water to halt cooking process. You can peel cooled eggs immediately or refrigerate unpeeled.

Poached Eggs

Hope Comerford

Makes 6–8 servings

1 cup water
4 large eggs

1. Place the trivet in the bottom of the inner pot of the Instant Pot and pour in the water.

2. You will need small silicone egg poacher cups that will fit in your Instant Pot to hold the eggs. Spray each silicone cup with nonstick cooking spray.

3. Crack each egg and pour it into the prepared cup.

4. Very carefully place the silicone cups into the Inner Pot so they do not spill.

5. Secure the lid by locking it into place and turn the vent to the sealing position.

6. Push the Steam button and adjust the time—2 minutes for a very runny egg all the way to 5 minutes for a slightly runny egg.

7. When the timer beeps, release the pressure manually and remove the lid, being very careful not to let the condensation in the lid drip into your eggs.

8. Very carefully remove the silicone cups from the inner pot.

9. Carefully remove the poached eggs from each silicone cup and serve immediately.

Baked Eggs

Esther J. Mast

Make 8 servings

1 cup water

2 tablespoons no-trans-fat tub margarine, melted

1 cup reduced-fat buttermilk baking mix

1½ cups fat-free cottage cheese

2 teaspoons chopped onion

1 teaspoon dried parsley

½ cup grated reduced-fat cheddar cheese

1 egg, slightly beaten

1¼ cups egg substitute

1 cup fat-free milk

Serving suggestion:

Serve with low-carb, low-sugar muffins and a fresh fruit cup.

1. Place the steaming rack into the bottom of the inner pot and pour in water.

2. Grease a round springform pan that will fit into the inner pot of the Instant Pot.

3. Pour melted margarine into springform pan.

4. Mix together buttermilk baking mix, cottage cheese, onion, parsley, cheese, egg, egg substitute, and milk in large mixing bowl.

5. Pour mixture over melted margarine. Stir slightly to distribute margarine.

6. Place the springform pan onto the steaming rack, close the lid, and secure to the locking position. Be sure the vent is turned to sealing. Set for 20 minutes on Manual at high pressure.

7. Let the pressure release naturally.

8. Carefully remove the springform pan with the handles of the steaming rack and allow to stand 10 minutes before cutting and serving.

Apple Oatmeal

Frances B. Musser

Makes 6 servings

2 cups water, divided

2 cups fat-free milk

1½ tablespoons honey

1 tablespoon light, soft tub margarine

¼ teaspoon salt

1 teaspoon cinnamon

2 cups dry rolled oats

1 cup chopped apples

½ cup chopped walnuts

1 tablespoon brown sugar

Brown sugar substitute to equal ½ tablespoon sugar

1. Place the steaming rack into the inner pot of the Instant pot and pour in 1 cup of water.

2. In an approximately 7-cup heat-safe baking dish, add all of your ingredients, including remaining 1 cup of water, and stir.

3. Place the dish on top of the steaming rack, close the lid, and secure it to a locking position.

4. Be sure the vent is set to sealing, then set the Instant Pot for 8 minutes on Manual on high pressure.

5. When it is done cooking, allow the pressure to release naturally for 5 minutes and then perform a quick release.

6. Carefully remove the rack and dish from the Instant Pot and serve.

Oatmeal Morning

Barbara Forrester Landis

Makes 6 servings

2 cups water, divided

2 cups uncooked steel-cut oats

1 cup dried cranberries

1 cup walnuts

½ teaspoon salt

1 tablespoon cinnamon

2 cups fat-free milk

1. Place the steaming rack into the inner pot of the Instant pot and pour in 1 cup of water.

2. In an approximately 7-cup heat-safe baking dish, add all of your ingredients, including the remaining 1 cup of water, and stir.

3. Place the dish on top of the steaming rack, close the lid, and secure it to a locking position.

4. Be sure the vent is set to sealing, then set the Instant Pot for 4 minutes on Manual on high pressure.

5. When it is done cooking, allow the pressure to release naturally.

6. Carefully remove the rack and dish from the Instant Pot and serve.

Best Steel-Cut Oats

Colleen Heatwole

Makes 4 servings

1 cup steel-cut oats

2 cups water

1 cup almond milk

Pinch salt

½ teaspoon vanilla extract

1 cinnamon stick

¼ cup raisins

¼ cup dried cherries

1 teaspoon ground cinnamon

¼ cup toasted almonds

Sweetener of choice, optional

1. Add all ingredients listed to the inner pot of the Instant Pot except the toasted almonds and sweetener.

2. Secure the lid and make sure the vent is turned to sealing. Cook 3 minutes on high, using Manual function.

3. Let the pressure release naturally.

4. Remove cinnamon stick.

5. Add almonds, and sweetener if desired, and serve.

Fruit Breakfast Cobbler

Hope Comerford

Makes 4 servings

2 pears, chopped

2 sweet apples, chopped

2 peaches, diced

2 tablespoons maple syrup

3 tablespoons coconut oil

1 teaspoon ground cinnamon

½ cup unsweetened
shredded coconut

½ cup pecans, diced

2 tablespoons flaxseed

¼ cup oats

1. Place the pears, apples, and peaches in the inner pot of your Instant Pot, then top with the maple syrup, coconut oil, and cinnamon. Lock lid and set vent to sealing.

2. Press Steam and set to 8 minutes.

3. When cook time is up, do a quick release. When lid is able to be removed, remove the fruit with a slotted spoon and place in a bowl. You want to leave the juices in the inner pot.

4. Set the Instant Pot to Sauté and put in the shredded coconut, pecan pieces, flaxseed, and oats. Stir them constantly, until the shredded coconut is lightly toasted.

5. Spoon the shredded coconut/oat mixture over the steamed fruit and enjoy.

Serving suggestion:

This is very good with a little bit of whipped cream on top, or even as a dessert with some vanilla ice cream.

Cynthia's Yogurt

Cynthia Hockman-Chupp

Makes 16 servings

1 gallon 2% milk

¼ cup yogurt with active cultures

1. Pour milk into the inner pot of the Instant Pot.

2. Lock lid, move vent to sealing, and press the yogurt button. Press Adjust until it reads "boil."

3. When boil cycle is complete (about 1 hour), check the temperature. It should be at 185°F. If it's not, use the sauté function to warm to 185°F.

4. After it reaches 185°F, unplug Instant Pot, remove inner pot, and cool. You can place on cooling rack and let it slowly cool. If in a hurry, submerge the base of the pot in cool water. Cool milk to 110°F.

5. When mixture reaches 110°F, stir in the ¼ cup of yogurt. Lock the lid in place and move vent to sealing.

6. Press Yogurt. Use the Adjust button until the screen says 8:00. This will now incubate for 8 hours.

7. After 8 hours (when the cycle is finished), chill yogurt, or go immediately to straining in step 8.

8. After chilling, or following the 8 hours, strain the yogurt using a nut milk bag. This will give it the consistency of Greek yogurt.

Serving suggestion:

When serving, top with fruit, granola, or nuts. If you'd like, add a dash of vanilla extract, peanut butter, or other flavoring. We also use this yogurt in smoothies!

Apple Butter

Hope Comerford

Makes 6 cups

5 pounds apples (about 15), peeled, cored, and sliced

½ cup brown sugar

¼ teaspoon ground cloves

½ teaspoon ground nutmeg

1 tablespoon cinnamon

Pinch salt

2 tablespoons lemon juice

1 tablespoon vanilla extract

¼ cup water

1. Combine all of the ingredients in the inner pot of the Instant Pot and mix well.

2. Lock the lid in place; turn the vent to sealing.

3. Press Manual and set to 60 minutes on high pressure.

4. When cooking time is over, let the steam release naturally.

5. Using an immersion blender, blend the apples until smooth.

Cinnamon French Toast Casserole

Hope Comerford

Makes 8 servings

3 eggs

2 cups milk

¼ cup maple syrup

1 teaspoon vanilla extract

1 teaspoon cinnamon

Pinch salt

1 (16-oz) loaf cinnamon swirl bread, cubed and left out overnight to go stale

1½ cups water

Serving suggestion:

Serve with whipped cream and fresh fruit on top, with an extra sprinkle of cinnamon.

1. In a medium sized bowl, whisk together the eggs, milk, maple syrup, vanilla, cinnamon, and salt. Stir in the cubes of cinnamon swirl bread.

2. You will need a 7-inch round pan for this. Spray the inside with nonstick spray, then pour the bread mixture into the pan.

3. Place the trivet in the bottom of the inner pot, then pour in the water.

4. Make foil sling and insert it onto the trivet. Carefully place the 7-inch pan on top of the foil sling/trivet.

5. Secure the lid to the locked position, then make sure the vent is turned to sealing.

6. Press the Manual button and use the "+/-" button to set the Instant Pot for 20 minutes on high pressure.

7. When cook time is up, let the Instant Pot release naturally for 5 minutes, then quick release the rest.

Quick and Easy Cinnamon Rolls

Hope Comerford

Makes 5 servings

2 cups water

1 (17½-oz) can Pillsbury Grands! Original Cinnamon Rolls with Icing

1. Place water in the inner pot of the Instant Pot, then place the trivet inside.

2. Cover the trivet with aluminum foil so that it also kind of wraps up the sides.

3. Grease a 7-inch round pan and arrange the cinnamon rolls inside. Set the icing aside. Place this pan on top of the aluminum foil inside the inner pot.

4. Secure the lid and make sure vent is on sealing. Press Manual, high pressure for 13 minutes.

5. Release the pressure manually when cooking time is up.

6. Remove the lid carefully so that the moisture does not drip on the cinnamon rolls.

7. Drizzle the icing on top of the cinnamon rolls and serve.

Steamed Brown Bread

Carolyn Spohn

Makes about 10 servings

1 cup rye flour

1 cup cornmeal

½ cup whole wheat flour

½ cup all-purpose flour

½ teaspoon salt

2 teaspoons baking soda

2 teaspoons cream of tartar

½ cup molasses

2 cups sour milk or buttermilk

1 cup raisins, optional

2 cups water

Serving suggestion:

Very good with baked beans for an old-fashioned New England dinner.

1. Prepare molds by generously greasing 4 pint-sized wide mouth canning jars or 3 of the larger cans from canned fruit. You will need lids and rings for the jars.

2. Mix all dry ingredients thoroughly in a bowl.

3. Mix the molasses and sour milk in a separate, larger bowl.

4. Add dry ingredients to the liquid ingredients and beat well.

5. Place rack in bottom of Instant Pot inner pot and add the water.

6. Fill prepared jars about ⅔ full and cover tightly with greased foil. Place the inner pot on rack.

7. Secure the lid and make sure vent is set to sealing. Press the Steam function and set for 30 minutes on high pressure.

8. Release pressure manually when cooking time is over, then carefully remove jars from cooker.

Boston Brown Bread

David Murphy

Makes 3 loaves

2 tablespoons butter, softened

¼ cup sugar

1 large egg, beaten

½ cup dark molasses

2 cups sprouted whole wheat flour

1 cup whole wheat baking flour

½ teaspoon salt

1 teaspoon baking soda

½ teaspoon baking powder

1 cup milk

½ cup dried fruits, like dates, raisins, cranberries, and currants

2 cups water

1. Cream together butter and sugar. Add egg and molasses and mix well. Sift in the flours, salt, baking soda, and baking powder. As you add dry ingredients, alternate with the milk. Once done, fold in the mixed dried fruits.

2. Spray down the inside of three 15¼-ounce cans (you can use soup cans) and the inside of three pieces of aluminum foil that have been shaped in the form of the cans (to be used as lids) with nonstick spray.

3. Evenly distribute the dough between the cans. Fill them up about 80 percent of the way. Leave about ½ inch of space from the top. Place the pieces of foil on top of the cans, lightly. We are just stopping excess moisture from entering the can.

4. Add water to your pot, and then insert the trivet into the bottom. Add the cans of dough. Lock the lid and close the vent. Cook on Manual at high pressure for 45 minutes and allow pressure to release naturally.

5. Allow to cool then remove from can to serve.

Rustic Bread

David Murphy

Makes 1 loaf

2 cups all-purpose flour

1 cup white whole wheat flour

2 teaspoons sea salt

½ teaspoon fast-acting yeast

1½ cups lukewarm water

1. In a large bowl, add all ingredients and mix well. Turn onto a piece of parchment paper. Place in your pot. Press Yogurt setting for 3½ to 4 hours.

2. Preheat oven to 425°F.

3. Time to remove dough. Your dough is going to be tacky! You will need to use floured hands. Remove dough from pot, peel off parchment paper, and place on a lightly floured surface. You want to form a nice ball shape. Dust it with flour, and cut a few slices in it with a sharp knife to add a little design to the top.

4. Place on a baking sheet, or place in a preheated Dutch oven. Then bake in the oven for approximately 25 minutes, or until a golden-brown color. Remove from oven and allow to cool.

Jalapeño Bacon Corn Bread

David Murphy

Makes 1 loaf

1 cup water

1 cup yellow cornmeal +
extra for dusting

¾ cup all-purpose flour

2 teaspoons baking powder

1 teaspoon salt

1⅓ cups grated sharp
cheddar cheese

2–3 jalapeño peppers,
seeded and finely chopped

½ cup creamed corn

¼ cup green scallions, thinly
sliced

¾ cup buttermilk

¼ cup butter, melted

¼ cup honey

2 eggs

8 strips cooked bacon, diced

Serving suggestion:

Serve with the Jalapeño
Peach Jam (page 54).

1. Add water to the Pot and place trivet into bottom. Grease and lightly coat a 7-inch cake pan with just a bit of cornmeal.

2. In a large mixing bowl, combine the 1 cup cornmeal, flour, baking powder, and salt. Mix well with a whisk.

3. Add the grated cheese, chopped jalapeño, creamed corn, and scallions to the flour mixture. Mix gently until well coated.

4. In a separate bowl, whisk together the buttermilk, melted butter, honey, and eggs. Pour over mixed dry ingredients and stir until just combined.

5. Once combined, add bacon and gently fold into corn bread mixture.

6. Pour into your cake pan. Cover the cake pan with a piece of aluminum foil. Place the cake pan on the trivet. Lock lid and close vent. Cook on Manual at high pressure for 24 minutes and release pressure naturally.

7. Place under a broiler for 2 minutes to brown the top.

Morning Bread

David Murphy

Makes 2 mini loaves

½ cup granulated sugar

2 large eggs

1 teaspoon vanilla extract

1 cup vegetable oil

1 large zucchini, peeled and grated

1 cup carrots, peeled and grated

1 cup crushed pineapple, drained

½ currants or raisins

2 cups all-purpose flour

1 teaspoon ground cinnamon

1 teaspoon baking powder

½ teaspoon baking soda

½ teaspoon sea salt

2 cups warm water

1. In a large bowl, combine sugar and eggs. Mix well. Then add vanilla, oil, zucchini, carrots, crushed pineapple, and currants.

2. In another bowl, add all dry ingredients and mix well with a whisk. Slowly add dry ingredients to wet ingredients.

3. Lightly spray a 7-cup pudding mold with nonstick spray. Pour batter into mold. Add warm water to your pot and insert trivet to bottom. Place mold on trivet and lightly cover with aluminum foil. Lock lid and close vent. Cook on Manual at high pressure for 40 minutes and release pressure naturally (approximately 20 to 25 minutes).

4. Allow to cool and then serve.

Chinese Steamed Buns

David Murphy

Makes 2 dozen

1 tablespoon active dry yeast

1 teaspoon sugar + 2 tablespoons

2¾ cups warm water, divided

1¾ cup all-purpose flour

Pinch sea salt

½ teaspoon baking powder

1 tablespoon vegetable oil

1. Mix together yeast, 1 teaspoon sugar, and ¼ cup warm water. Allow to stand for 30 minutes.

2. Add in ½ cup warm water, flour, salt, 2 tablespoons sugar, baking powder, and vegetable oil.

3. Knead dough until all is smooth and very elastic. Add flour as needed if tacky. Cover and allow to sit for approximately 3 hours. You want your dough to almost triple in size.

4. Once dough is done, punch in the middle. Bring onto a lightly floured surface and knead for a couple of minutes. Then cut the dough in half and roll into 2 long logs. With a pastry knife or blade, cut into 2-inch pieces. You should yield a total of 2 dozen. Place each one on a piece of wax paper that has been cut into 2 x 2-inch squares.

5. Add 2 cups of water to your pot. Press Sauté and heat until water is almost boiling. Place trivet into pot. Place 5 to 6 pieces of dough into your Instant Pot steamer basket, and place on trivet. Lock lid and close vent. Cook on Manual at high pressure for approximately 16 minutes.

6. When removing lid, remove at an angle as to not drip water on your buns. Remove steamer basket and repeat for remaining buns.

Easy Morning Frittata

David Murphy

Makes 6–8 servings

1 cup water

8 large eggs

½ cup milk

½ cup flour

Sea salt to taste

Cracked pepper to taste

1 large red pepper, diced into small cubes

1 cup tomatoes, sliced or chopped

½ cup baby kale, sliced thin

1½ cups shredded Colby Jack cheese

1. Put trivet in the bottom of the pot and add water.

2. In a bowl, whisk eggs, milk, flour, salt, and pepper. Add veggies and 1 cup of cheese until combined.

3. Pour the mixture into a 7-inch cake pan or other dish that will fit, lightly coated with nonstock spray. Cover the top with foil and place on top of the trivet.

4. Lock the lid and close the vent. Cook for 30 minutes on Manual at high pressure.

5. Once done, let pressure naturally release for 10 minutes. Then quick pressure release the remaining pressure.

6. Remove frittata from pot, and sprinkle the top with the remaining cheese. Place foil back on top to help melt the cheese.

Easy Quiche

Becky Bontrager Horst

Makes 6 servings, 1 slice per serving

1 cup water

¼ cup chopped onion

¼ cup chopped mushroom, optional

3 ounces 75%-less-fat cheddar cheese, shredded

2 tablespoons bacon bits, chopped ham, or browned sausage

4 eggs

¼ teaspoon salt

1½ cups fat-free milk

½ cup whole wheat flour

1 tablespoon trans-fat-free tub margarine

1. Pour water into Instant Pot and place the steaming rack inside.

2. Spray a 6-inch round cake pan with nonstick spray.

3. Sprinkle the onion, mushroom, shredded cheddar, and meat around in the cake pan.

4. Combine remaining ingredients in medium bowl. Pour over meat and vegetables mixture.

5. Place the cake pan onto the steaming rack, close the lid and secure to the locking position. Be sure the vent is turned to sealing. Set for 25 minutes on Manual at high pressure.

6. Let the pressure release naturally.

7. Carefully remove the cake pan with the handles of the steaming rack and allow to stand 10 minutes before cutting and serving.

Potato-Bacon Gratin

Valerie Drobel

Makes 8 servings, about 5 ounces per serving

1 tablespoon olive oil

1 (6-oz) bag fresh spinach

1 clove garlic, minced

4 large potatoes, peeled or unpeeled

6 ounces Canadian bacon slices

5 ounces reduced-fat grated Swiss cheddar

1 cup lower-sodium, lower-fat chicken broth

2 cups water

1. Set the Instant Pot to Sauté and pour in the olive oil. Cook the spinach and garlic in olive oil just until spinach is wilted (5 minutes or less). Turn off the instant pot.

2. Cut potatoes into thin slices about ¼ inch thick.

3. Spray a springform pan that fits into the inner pot of your Instant Pot with nonstick spray, then layer ⅓ the potatoes, ½ the bacon, ⅓ the cheese, and half the wilted spinach.

4. Repeat layers ending with potatoes. Reserve ⅓ cheese for later.

5. Pour chicken broth over everything.

6. Wipe the bottom of your Instant Pot to soak up any remaining oil, then add water and the steaming rack. Place the springform pan on top.

7. Close the lid and secure to the locking position. Be sure the vent is turned to sealing. Set for 35 minutes on Manual at high pressure.

8. Perform a quick release.

9. Top with the remaining cheese, then allow to stand 10 minutes before removing from the Instant Pot, cutting, and serving.

Southwestern Egg Casserole

Eileen Eash

Makes 12 servings

1 cup water

2½ cups egg substitute

½ cup flour

1 teaspoon baking powder

⅛ teaspoon salt

⅛ teaspoon pepper

2 cups fat-free cottage cheese

1½ cups shredded 75%-less-fat sharp cheddar cheese

¼ cup no-trans-fat tub margarine, melted

2 (4-oz) cans chopped green chilies

1. Place the steaming rack into the bottom of the inner pot and pour in water.

2. Grease a round springform pan that will fit into the inner pot of the Instant Pot.

3. Combine the egg substitute, flour, baking powder, salt and pepper in a mixing bowl. It will be lumpy.

4. Stir in the cottage cheese, cheddar cheese, margarine, and green chilies then pour into the springform pan.

5. Place the springform pan onto the steaming rack, close the lid, and secure to the locking position. Be sure the vent is turned to sealing. Set for 20 minutes on Manual at high pressure.

6. Let the pressure release naturally.

7. Carefully remove the springform pan with the handles of the steaming rack and allow to stand 10 minutes before cutting and serving.

Shredded Potato Omelet

Mary H. Nolt

Makes 6 servings

3 slices bacon, cooked and crumbled

2 cups shredded cooked potatoes

¼ cup minced onion

¼ cup minced green bell pepper

1 cup egg substitute

¼ cup fat-free milk

¼ teaspoon salt

⅛ teaspoon black pepper

1 cup 75%-less-fat shredded cheddar cheese

1 cup water

1. With nonstick cooking spray, spray the inside of a round baking dish that will fit in your Instant Pot inner pot.

2. Sprinkle the bacon, potatoes, onion, and bell pepper around the bottom of the baking dish.

3. Mix together the egg substitute, milk, salt, and pepper in mixing bowl. Pour over potato mixture.

4. Top with cheese.

5. Add water to the inner pot, place the steaming rack into the bottom, and place the round baking dish on top.

6. Close the lid and secure to the locking position. Be sure the vent is turned to sealing. Set for 20 minutes on Manual at high pressure.

7. Let the pressure release naturally.

8. Carefully remove the baking dish with the handles of the steaming rack and allow to stand 10 minutes before cutting and serving.

Appetizers, Dips & Sauces

Game Day Pizza Dip

David Murphy

Makes 8 servings

8 ounces cream cheese, room temperature

½ cup spaghetti sauce or pizza sauce (I used basil flavored)

1 cup shredded mozzarella cheese

½ teaspoon chopped basil

2 cups water

1. Place the block of room temperature cream cheese into the bottom of a 7-cup Pyrex dish and spread out as evenly as you can with the back of a spoon.

2. Add layer of sauce, and spread around evenly. Sprinkle mozzarella cheese around to create an even coating, then sprinkle the basil on top. (You don't have to add basil, but I love the freshness it adds.)

3. Add water into the inner pot and place the steaming rack inside. Please make sure the inner pot is inside of your Instant Pot before you pour water into it!

4. Place the Pyrex dish full of pizza dip ingredients onto the steaming rack. Lock the lid and close the vent. Place on Manual at high pressure for 20 minutes.

5. Once done, do a quick release. Remove lid at angle so that the moisture droplets from the lid doesn't pour into the pizza dip.

6. Allow the steaming rack handles to cool for a minute or two before removing from the Instant Pot.

Buffalo Chicken Dip

Hope Comerford

Makes 26 servings

2 large frozen boneless skinless chicken breasts

¾ cup Frank's RedHot sauce

½ cup sodium-free chicken broth

1 cup light ranch dressing

2 (8-oz) packages fat-free cream cheese, softened

1½ cups reduced-fat shredded cheddar jack cheese

1. Place the frozen chicken, hot sauce, and chicken broth into the inner pot of the Instant Pot. Secure the lid and make sure the vent is set to sealing.

2. Set the Instant Pot for 10 minutes on Manual on high pressure. When cooking time is over, let the pressure release naturally for 10 minutes and then perform a quick release.

3. Remove the lid and press Cancel. Then choose Sauté low.

4. Stir in the ranch dressing, cream cheese, and cheddar jack cheese. Cook, stirring until well blended and warm.

Serving suggestion:

Serve with whole grain tortilla chips.

Spinach and Artichoke Dip

Michele Ruvola

Makes 10–12 servings

8 ounces cream cheese

1 (10-oz.) box frozen spinach

½ cup chicken broth

1 (14-oz.) can artichoke
hearts, drained

½ cup sour cream

½ cup mayo

3 cloves garlic, minced

1 teaspoon onion powder

16 ounces shredded
Parmesan cheese

8 ounces shredded
mozzarella

1. Put all ingredients in the inner pot of the Instant
Pot, except the Parmesan cheese and the mozzarella
cheese.

2. Secure the lid and set vent to sealing. Place on
Manual at high pressure for 4 minutes.

3. Do a quick release of steam.

4. Immediately stir in the cheeses.

Serving suggestion:

Serve with vegetables, sliced
bread, or chips.

Creamy Spinach Dip

Jessica Stoner

Makes 10–12 servings

8 ounces cream cheese

1 cup sour cream

10 ounces frozen spinach

½ cup finely chopped onion

½ cup vegetable broth

5 cloves garlic, minced

½ teaspoon salt

¼ teaspoon black pepper

12 ounces shredded Monterey Jack cheese

12 ounces shredded Parmesan cheese

1. Add cream cheese, sour cream, spinach, onion, vegetable broth, garlic, salt, and pepper to the inner pot of the Instant Pot.

2. Secure lid, make sure vent is set to sealing, and set to the Bean/Chili setting on high pressure for 5 minutes.

3. When done, do a manual release.

4. Add the cheeses and mix well until creamy and well combined.

Serving suggestion:

Serve with tortilla chips or bread.

Creamy Jalapeño Chicken Dip

Hope Comerford

Makes 10 servings

1 pound boneless chicken breast

8 ounces cream cheese

3 jalapeños, seeded and sliced

½ cup water

8 ounces shredded cheddar cheese

¾ cup sour cream

1. Place the chicken, cream cheese, jalapeños, and water in the inner pot of the Instant Pot.

2. Secure the lid so it's locked and turn the vent to sealing.

3. Press Manual and set the Instant Pot for 12 minutes on high pressure.

4. When cooking time is up, turn off Instant Pot, do a quick release of the remaining pressure, then remove lid.

5. Shred the chicken between 2 forks, either in the pot or on a cutting board, then place back in the inner pot.

6. Stir in the shredded cheese and sour cream. Enjoy!

Hummus

Colleen Heatwole

Makes 8 servings

1 cup dry garbanzo beans (chickpeas)

4 cups water

2 tablespoons fresh lemon juice

¼ cup chopped onion

3 cloves garlic, minced

½ cup tahini (sesame paste)

2 teaspoons cumin

2 teaspoons olive oil

Pinch cayenne pepper

½ teaspoon salt

Serving suggestion:

I serve with vegetable crudités, pita, or any crackers I have on hand.

1. Place garbanzo beans and water into inner pot of Instant Pot. Secure lid and make sure vent is set to sealing.

2. Cook garbanzo beans in water for 40 minutes using the Manual setting at high pressure.

3. When cooking time is up, let the pressure release naturally.

4. Test the garbanzos. If still firm, cook using slow-cooker function until they are soft.

5. Drain the garbanzo beans, but save ½ cup of the cooking liquid.

6. Combine the garbanzos, lemon juice, onion, garlic, tahini, cumin, oil, pepper, and salt in a blender or food processor.

7. Puree until smooth, adding chickpea liquid as needed to thin the purée. Taste and adjust seasonings accordingly.

Blackberry Baked Brie

Hope Comerford

Makes 4–6 servings

1 (8-oz.) round Brie

1 cup water

¼ cup blackberry preserves

2 teaspoons chopped fresh mint

1. Slice a grid pattern into the top of the rind of the Brie with a knife.

2. In a 7-inch round baking dish, place the Brie, then cover the baking dish securely with foil.

3. Insert the trivet into the inner pot of the Instant Pot; pour in the water.

4. Make a foil sling and arrange it on top of the trivet. Place the baking dish on top of the trivet and foil sling.

5. Secure the lid to the locked position and turn the vent to sealing.

6. Press Manual and set the Instant Pot for 15 minutes on high pressure.

7. When cooking time is up, turn off the Instant Pot and do a quick release of the pressure.

8. When the valve has dropped, remove the lid, then remove the baking dish.

9. Remove the top rind of the Brie and top with the preserves. Sprinkle with the fresh mint.

Serving suggestion:

Serve with crostini, baguettes, or crackers. (Rice crackers are my favorite with this.)

Root Beer Chicken Wings

Hope Comerford

Makes 15–18 servings

5 pounds chicken wings, tips removed and separated at joint

1 can (12-oz.) root beer + ¼ cup

¼ cup brown sugar

½ teaspoon red pepper flakes

1. Place all the chicken wing pieces into the inner pot of the Instant Pot. Pour the can of root beer over the top.

2. Secure the lid and turn the vent to sealing.

3. Press Manual and set the Instant Pot to 18 minutes on high pressure.

4. Preheat the oven on broil.

5. When cooking time is up, turn off the Instant Pot and do a quick release of the pressure.

6. Remove the wings and spread them out on a baking sheet.

7. Mix together the ¼ cup root beer, brown sugar, and red pepper flakes. Brush this over the wings.

8. Place the wings under the broiler for 2 minutes.

Levi's Sesame Chicken Wings

Shirley Unternahrer Hinh

Makes 16 appetizer servings

1 cup water

3 pounds chicken wings

1 cup sugar substitute to equal 6 tablespoons sugar

¾ cup light soy sauce

½ cup no-salt-added ketchup

2 tablespoons canola oil

2 tablespoons sesame oil

2 cloves garlic, minced

Salt to taste

Pepper to taste

Toasted sesame seeds

1. Place the trivet in the Instant Pot inner pot with water. Carefully place the chicken wings on top of the trivet.

2. Seal the lid and make sure vent is set to sealing. Set the Instant Pot to Manual for 10 minutes on high pressure.

3. While the wings are cooking, simmer the remaining ingredients, except the sesame seeds, in a small saucepan.

4. When cook time is up, let the pressure release naturally for 5 minutes, then perform a quick release of the remaining pressure.

5. Meanwhile, line a baking sheet with foil and place a baking rack on top. Turn the oven on to broil.

6. Carefully remove about half of the wings into a bowl and pour half of the sauce over the top. Gently stir to coat them, then place them on top of the baking rack. Repeat this process with the remaining wings and sauce.

7. Broil the wings about 5 inches from top of the oven for 5 minutes.

8. Sprinkle sesame seeds over top just before serving.

Smokey Barbecue Meatballs

Carla Koslowsky, Sherry Kreider, Jennie Martin

Makes 10 servings, 1 meatball per serving

1½ pounds 90%-lean ground beef

½ cup quick oats

½ cup fat-free evaporated milk or milk

¼ cup egg substitute

¼–½ cup finely chopped onion, optional

¼ teaspoon garlic powder

¼ teaspoon pepper

¼ teaspoon chili powder

1 teaspoon salt

2 tablespoons olive oil

Sauce

1½ cups ketchup

6 tablespoons Splenda Brown Sugar Blend

¼ cup chopped onion

¼ teaspoon liquid smoke

1. Mix ground beef, oats, milk, egg substitute, onion, garlic powder, pepper, chili powder, and salt together. Form 10 balls, each weighing about 2 ounces.

2. Set the Instant Pot to Sauté and pour the olive oil into the inner pot. Once warm, add in the meatballs one at a time. Just try to make sure they're lightly browned on at least two sides. Turn the Instant Pot off by pressing Cancel.

3. Remove the meatballs onto a paper towel-lined plate and wipe the inner pot mostly clean of bits of meat and oil. Put the meatballs back into the inner pot.

4. Mix the sauce ingredients in a small bowl then pour them over the meatballs.

5. Secure the lid and make sure the vent is set to sealing. Cook on the Manual setting for 4 minutes on high pressure.

6. When cooking time is up, perform a quick release of the pressure. Serve and enjoy!

Meatballs

Carol Eveleth

Makes about 16 meatballs

2 pounds ground beef

1½ cups chopped onions

1½ cups bread crumbs

2 teaspoons salt

½ teaspoon black pepper

2½ tablespoons Worcestershire sauce

3 eggs

1 (8-oz.) can tomato sauce

1 cup water

3½ tablespoons vinegar

3½ tablespoons brown sugar

2½ tablespoons mustard

1 tablespoon liquid smoke

2 tablespoons olive oil

Serving suggestion:

Serve meatballs with barbecue sauce, if desired.

1. Combine all ingredients, except the olive oil, in a medium bowl and mix thoroughly by hand.

2. Form into approximately 26 two-inch meatballs.

3. Coat the bottom of the Instant Pot inner pot with oil. If you wish to brown the meatballs, turn on the Sauté function and brown on all sides, or brown in a separate nonstick pan first.

5. Layer the browned or raw meatballs in the inner pot, leaving ½ inch of space between them. Don't press down.

6. Secure the lid and make sure vent is set to sealing. Set the Instant Pot to Manual and select low pressure. Set the cook time to 10 minutes.

7. Once the timer goes off, manually release the pressure.

8. Remove the lid and serve the meatballs.

Porcupine Meatballs

Carolyn Spohn

Makes about 8 meatballs

1 pound ground beef or turkey

½ cup raw long-grain white rice

1 egg

¼ cup finely minced onion

1 or 2 cloves garlic, minced

¼ teaspoon dried basil and/or oregano, optional

1 (10¾-oz.) can condensed tomato soup

½ soup can water

1. Mix all ingredients, except tomato soup and water, in a bowl to combine well.

2. Form into balls about 1½ inches in diameter.

3. Mix tomato soup and water in the inner pot of the Instant Pot, then add the meatballs.

4. Secure the lid and make sure the vent is turned to sealing.

5. Press the Meat button and set for 10 minutes on high pressure.

6. Allow the pressure to release naturally after cook time is up.

Serving suggestion:

Very good on pasta or noodles with green salad and crusty bread.

Swedish Meatballs

David Murphy

Makes 6 servings

Meatballs

1½ pounds ground beef (90% lean)
½ cup panko bread crumbs
½ cup milk
1 medium Vidalia sweet onion, diced fine
1 teaspoon sea salt
½ teaspoon cracked pepper
¼ teaspoon allspice
¼ teaspoon nutmeg
1 teaspoon garlic powder
1 egg, beaten
2 tablespoons olive oil

Sauce

2½ cups beef broth
6 tablespoons salted butter
1 teaspoon Dijon mustard
1 teaspoon Worcestershire sauce
2 cups heavy cream, divided
¼ cup flour
1 tablespoon cornstarch

1. In a bowl, add all ingredients for the meatballs. Mix well with a wooden spoon or your hands. Form meatballs and set them on parchment paper. Make them the size of 50-cent pieces.

2. Turn on the pot's Sauté setting, and add olive oil. Once heated, add about 12 to 15 meatballs. You are going to sear on all sides until lightly browned. Remove meatballs and set to the side once done. You will have to work your meatballs in batches.

3. Add beef broth and stir to deglaze the pan. Add butter, Dijon mustard, Worcestershire sauce, and 1 cup of the heavy cream (reserve the remaining 1 cup). Stir well. Press the Cancel button.

4. Add the meatballs back into the pot. Lock the lid and close the vent.

5. Cook on Manual at high pressure for 6 minutes. Let pressure naturally release for 10 minutes. Quick release the remaining pressure.

6. Whisk remaining heavy cream with flour and cornstarch until there are no lumps. Remove meatballs and set to the side.

7. Press Sauté in Normal mode and mix in the flour/cream mixture. Bring to a simmer, stirring frequently, until thickened. Once thickened, press Cancel.

8. Add meatballs back in and give a gentle stir.

"Easier than I Thought" Pickles

David Murphy

Makes 2 quarts

1 pound Kirby cucumbers, halved lengthwise and tips cut off

¾ cup fresh dill sprigs

1 cup warm water

½ cup distilled white vinegar

¼ cup sugar

2 tablespoons kosher salt

1 teaspoon whole coriander seeds

1 teaspoon dill seeds

1½ cups water, room temperature

1. Into a quart-sized sterilized jar, add the cucumber halves and fresh dill.

2. In a small bowl, combine the remaining ingredients except the 1½ cups water at room temperature. Stir until the sugar and salt have dissolved. Once dissolved, pour into the jar over the cucumbers.

3. Add 1½ cups water to your pot, and place trivet in the bottom. Place lid on jar (finger tight). Lock lid and close vent.

4. Place on Manual at high pressure for 5 minutes. Once done, quick release pressure and remove lid. Allow jar to cool for 5 to 10 minutes before removing. Allow to cool to room temperature.

5. Place in the fridge for a minimum of 24 hours before enjoying.

Sauerkraut

David Murphy

Makes approximately 1 quart

1 medium head cabbage

2 tablespoons sea salt

1. Shred cabbage into thin strips. Sprinkle with sea salt.

2. Add to Instant Pot and knead the cabbage with hands, or pound with a wooden cabbage crusher about 10 to 12 minutes, until there is enough liquid to cover.

3. Place a weighted trivet or fermentation weight on top of the cabbage to ensure it stays underneath the liquid. If necessary, add a bit of water to completely cover cabbage.

4. Lock lid and close vent. Press Yogurt button with Less Heat. Run cycle for 5 days. Once every 24 hours, quick release any built-up pressure and remove lid to allow air back in.

5. After 5 days, transfer contents from your pot to a jar with a lid. Place in fridge for 2 days for optimal flavor; however, you can start eating it right away!

Easy-Peasy Kimchi

David Murphy

Makes approximately 2¼ cups

1 head Napa cabbage, cut into quarters or 2-inch wedges, depending on size of cabbage

1 daikon radish, peeled and sliced thin

½ cup sea salt

2 tablespoons minced garlic

2 tablespoons minced ginger

1 teaspoon sugar

4 tablespoons Korean red pepper flakes

1. Place cabbage and radish into your Instant Pot and sprinkle with sea salt. Mix thoroughly with your hands. Press Yogurt Less Heat function. Lock lid and close vent. Allow to sit for 2 hours.

2. Quick release any pressure that might have built up. Press Cancel when complete.

3. Thoroughly rinse your cabbage under cold running water. (We're trying to remove as much salt as we can.) Allow to sit in a colander to drain for at least 20 minutes.

4. Place cabbage back into your Instant Pot. Add all other remaining ingredients and mix well and slowly. We are trying to infuse the flavor of the Korean pepper flakes into your cabbage and radish. Press mixture firmly into pot. Place a steamer basket on top and add a little weight to help keep your mixture a little pressed. I used a round 7-cup Pyrex dish on top of a trivet to keep it weighted down.

5. Press Yogurt button Less Heat. Lock lid and close vent. Allow to sit for 3 to 4 days. Once every 24 hours, quick release any pressure that might have built up.

6. Remove lid, and firmly press cabbage into liquid. When fermentation is done, place in the fridge to chill and eat when you're ready.

Tomatillo "Chow Chow"

David Murphy

Makes approximately 2½ cups

2 pounds chopped tomatillos

1 red bell pepper, deseeded and sliced

2 jalapeño peppers, deseeded and sliced

2 cups Vidalia sweet onions, chopped

½ teaspoon sea salt

1 cup apple cider vinegar

½ cup granulated sugar

½ teaspoon crushed red pepper flakes

¼ teaspoon celery seed

1 tablespoon molasses

1. In a blender, add tomatillos, red bell pepper, jalapeño peppers, and onions. Pulse until finely chopped. Transfer to your pot. Stir in salt. Press Yogurt button Less Heat. Allow to sit overnight covered with the lid. You can leave the vent open.

2. Discard any liquid in the pot. You can use a wooden spoon to press liquid out. Add in all remaining ingredients. Press Sauté button. Allow mixture to come to a boil. Stir occasionally. You want the liquid in the pot to evaporate.

3. Transfer to jars with a lid. Allow to cool to room temperature. Transfer to the fridge.

Pickled Spiced Carrots

David Murphy

Makes 3 pints

3 pounds carrots

3 cloves garlic

3–4 jalapeños, sliced thin

7 dill sprigs

3½ cups white vinegar

¼ cup pickling salt

1½ cups water

1. Prepare carrots. Cut off tops and bottoms. You want to cut carrots into thick strips of about 4½ inches in length. I cut mine in half and then in half again.

2. Into a pint-sized sterilized jar, add the carrot strips, a clove of garlic, 8 to 10 slices of jalapeños, and fresh dill. Repeat this step with another jar to use up all the carrots, garlic, jalapeños, and dill.

3. In a small bowl, combine the white vinegar and pickling salt. Stir until the salt has dissolved. Once dissolved, pour into the jar over the carrot strips.

4. Add water to your pot, and place trivet into the bottom. Place lids on jars (finger tight). Lock lid and close vent.

5. Place on Manual at high pressure for 8 minutes. Once done, quick release pressure and remove lid. Allow jars to cool for 5 to 10 minutes before removing. Allow to cool to room temperature.

6. Place in the fridge for a minimum of 24 hours before eating.

Refrigerator Pickled Beets

Bryan Woolley

Serves: Variable

5–6 medium beets

2 cups water, divided

2 cinnamon sticks

5 whole cloves

1 large onion, thinly sliced

2 cups vinegar

½ cup sugar

1. Trim off beet greens and scrub beets thoroughly.

2. Place steam rack inside Instant Pot. Place cleaned beets on rack.

3. Pour 1 cup water into the Instant Pot. Secure lid.

4. Pressure cook on high for 15 minutes. Use quick-release method to release steam.

5. Let beets cool. Remove outer skins.

6. Slice beets into ½-inch cubes, placing them in a sealable container along with cinnamon sticks, whole cloves, and onion.

7. In a large bowl, whisk vinegar, 1 cup water, and sugar together until sugar has dissolved. Pour over beets. Cover and refrigerate overnight before serving.

8. Will keep about two weeks when refrigerated.

Pickled Eggs

Bryan Woolley

Serves: Variable

2 (1-quart) jars with lids, sterilized

24 large eggs

1 cup water

4 cups white vinegar

⅓ cup sugar

1 tablespoon yellow mustard seeds

1 tablespoon black peppercorns

2 tablespoons dry dill

4 bay leaves, crushed

1 medium onion, sliced

1 tablespoon seasoned salt

1. Set clean quart jars aside until ready to use. Place steam rack inside Instant Pot. Add eggs along with 1 cup water. Secure lid and set pressure to high. Cook 5 minutes. Allow pressure to release naturally.

2. Once steam has released, remove lid. Place eggs into bowl of cold water. Set aside.

3. Clean Instant Pot and add the white vinegar, sugar, yellow mustard seeds, black peppercorns, dry dill, crushed bay leaves, onion slices, and seasoned salt. Select Sauté mode, bringing mixture to a boil while stirring.

4. Once eggs have cooled sufficiently to handle, peel and divide them between the clean quart jars.

5. Divide and pour pickling solution between the two prepared jars.

6. If needed, strain remaining pickling solution and finish dividing the herbs and spices between the two jars. (Reserve any extra for a vinaigrette on a salad.)

7. Secure lids on jars. Refrigerate overnight. Keep jars in refrigerator when not using. Will last about two weeks.

8. Serve alone or with your favorite salad.

Deviled Eggs

Bryan Woolley

Makes 12 servings

1 cup water

12 large eggs

½ cup mayonnaise

¼ cup dill relish

2 teaspoons paprika

1 tablespoon yellow mustard, optional

2 teaspoons salt

1 tablespoon black pepper

Freshly chopped parsley or chives, optional

1. Place steam rack inside Instant Pot. Add water. Carefully place eggs onto steam rack. Secure lid and pressure cook eggs on high for 5 minutes.

2. Do a quick pressure release. (I like to place a clean kitchen towel over the steam vent to catch any hot water droplets that come out.)

3. Remove eggs and place them in a bowl of cold water to cool them.

4. Peel and slice eggs in half lengthwise, scooping egg yolks into a mixing bowl. Place egg white halves on baking sheet.

5. To the egg yolks, add mayonnaise, relish, paprika, mustard (optional), salt, and black pepper. Stir ingredients together until fully mixed.

6. Carefully spoon yolk mixture into center round of each egg white half.

7. Sprinkle prepared deviled eggs with freshly chopped parsley or chives, if using.

Deviled Eggs Squared

David Murphy

Makes 12

8 large eggs

1½ cups water

¼ cup mayonnaise

2 tablespoons yellow mustard

Sea salt to taste

Freshly ground black pepper
  to taste

Paprika to garnish

Scallions to garnish

1. Crack and separate the yolks from the whites into two mixing bowls. Set aside the yolks. Whip the whites just until frothy. Pour into a 3-cup Pyrex dish, and then cover with foil.

2. Whip egg yolks until blended, and set to the side.

3. Pour water into your pot and place trivet into bottom. Place your dish of egg whites inside, lock the lid, and close the vent. Put on Manual at high pressure for 6 minutes. Let pressure naturally release for 2 minutes, and then quick release the rest of the pressure.

4. Remove dish from the pot and allow to cool to room temperature. Once cooled, place in the fridge for 15 to 20 minutes. Drain water from your Instant Pot.

5. Turn machine on in Sauté mode and lightly spray bottom of inner pot with nonstick spray. Once hot, add yolks. You will want to constantly stir the egg yolks so you don't overcook them by accident—it's not fun having to start all over again.

6. Take out cooked egg yolks, and flake with a fork. Then add mayonnaise, mustard, salt, and pepper. Mix well with a fork. Place contents into a pastry bag. Place in fridge to cool for about 10 to 12 minutes.

(Continued on next page)

7. Retrieve the egg whites from the fridge. Remove egg whites from the dish and place on a cutting board. With a sharp knife, cut 2 equally spaced lines vertically, and then 4 equally spaced lines horizontally. You will wind up with 12 pieces.

8. With the pastry bag, create dollops of yolk mixture on top of each piece. Garnish with paprika and pieces of scallions. Place back in the fridge until ready to serve.

Applesauce

Hope Comerford

Makes 6 cups

5 pounds apples (whatever kind(s) you like), peeled, cored, and sliced

¼ cup water

2 teaspoons vanilla extract

3–4 tablespoons lemon juice

3 tablespoons brown sugar

¼ cup or less of white sugar

¼ teaspoon cinnamon

1. Place all of the ingredients into the inner pot of the Instant Pot and give a stir.

2. Secure the lid, making sure it locks and turn the vent to sealing.

3. Press the Manual button and set it for 5 minutes on high pressure.

4. When cooking time is up, let the pressure release naturally.

5. When pressure is done releasing, open lid, then use a potato smasher or immersion blender to make the applesauce as smooth or lumpy as you like.

Rhubarb Sauce

Esther Porter

Makes 6 servings

1½ pounds rhubarb

⅛ teaspoon salt

½ cup water

½ cup sugar

1. Cut rhubarb into ½-inch slices.

2. Combine all ingredients in Instant Pot. Press Slow Cook mode and cook on low 4 to 5 hours.

3. Serve chilled.

Variation:

Add 1 pint sliced strawberries about 30 minutes before removing from heat.

Rosé Marmalade

David Murphy

Makes approximately 3½ cups

4 pounds strawberries, room temperature, halved

2½ cups sugar

1 bottle decent rosé

Juice from 1 lemon

1 vanilla bean, split and seeded

1. Add all ingredients to your Instant Pot. Press the Sauté button and allow mixture to boil. Press Cancel and transfer marmalade to a storage container such as a bowl, and let cool completely.

2. Refrigerate overnight or up to two days.

3. Strain and reserve the liquid, setting the strawberries to the side. In your pot, boil the rosé syrup until the temperature hits 215°F and the liquid is reduced by about half, about 15 to 20 minutes. The best function to use is the Steam function—it keeps a nice heat going strong. If you use the Sauté button, you might come across an error message of "HOT" which means that it's overheating and will turn off automatically.

4. Carefully add the strawberries to the syrup and continue to boil, stirring frequently, until the mixture is thick, about 25 to 30 minutes. Check the temperature regularly. This marmalade has a soft set, so it will be ready at 212 to 215°F.

5. Remove the vanilla bean and pour strawberry content into jars. A canning funnel will work best. Seal with lids and place in the fridge to cool.

Everyday Peach Salsa

David Murphy

Makes approximately 3 pints

6 cups fresh peaches, peeled, pitted, and chopped

½ cup Vidalia sweet onion, chopped

½ cup red onion, chopped

½ cup red bell pepper, chopped

4 jalapeño peppers, minced

¼ cup chopped fresh cilantro

3 cloves garlic, minced

½ teaspoon ground cumin

1 tablespoon distilled white vinegar

1 teaspoon lime juice

1 teaspoon grated lime zest

1 package light fruit pectin crystals

1. Add all ingredients except pectin into your pot and press the Sauté button. Bring to a boil, and stir in pectin.

2. Boil for 1 minute, stirring constantly. Press Cancel and allow salsa to sit for 5 to 10 minutes to cool.

3. Transfer to three 1-pint sterilized jars, seal the lids, and place in the fridge to chill. Peach salsa for days!

Knee-Slappin' Bacon Jam

David Murphy

Makes approximately 2 cups

1 pound thick-cut bacon, diced into ½-inch pieces

1 tablespoon salted butter

3 large onions, halved and thinly sliced (about 4 cups)

1 tablespoon minced garlic

1 tablespoon horseradish

½ cup packed brown sugar

½ cup apple cider vinegar

1 tablespoon instant coffee

½ cup water

1. Put bacon in your Instant Pot. Select Sauté and adjust to Normal. Cook and stir until bacon is almost crisp. Press Cancel and remove bacon pieces to paper towel. Remove bacon grease from pot.

2. Select Sauté and adjust to Normal. Add butter. Once melted, add onions, garlic, and horseradish. Cook and stir for 5 minutes until just tender. Press Cancel.

3. Add brown sugar, apple cider vinegar, instant coffee, cooked bacon, and water. Stir to combine. Secure the lid on the pot. Close the valve. Cook on Manual at high pressure for 10 minutes.

4. Quick release the pressure. Remove lid. Use an immersion blender to break down ingredients to jam consistency. If you prefer it thicker, cook an additional 4 minutes on Sauté setting to reduce the liquid.

Jalapeño Peach Jam

David Murphy

Makes approximately 6½ pints

8–9 ripe peaches, peeled, pitted, and roughly chopped

2 jalapeño peppers, finely chopped or sliced

3 tablespoons lemon juice

1 tablespoon apple cider vinegar

5 cups sugar

½ teaspoon lemon zest

½ teaspoon grated ginger

3 tablespoons powdered pectin

1. Add all ingredients to your pot. Press the Sauté button and allow mixture to boil.

2. As the ingredients heat up, gently mash the peaches with a potato masher. Of course, if you want a smoother consistency, you can use an immersion blender. Press the Cancel button and wait 5 minutes.

3. Press the Steam button and bring your jam to a boil for about 8 to 12 minutes. Stir very often so it doesn't burn the bottom of your pot. If you want it a little thicker, continue to boil.

4. Press Cancel once you have your desired consistency. Pour contents into your favorite canning jars.

Orange-Honey Cranberry Sauce

Brittney Horst

Makes 6–8 servings

3 cups fresh cranberries

½ cup orange juice
(about 2 medium oranges)

½ cup 100% apple cider

1 tablespoon orange zest

Pinch pumpkin pie spice

¼ teaspoon salt

Sauté ingredients

¼ cup amaretto, optional

⅔ cup honey

1. Add the cranberries, orange juice, apple cider, orange zest, pumpkin pie spice, and salt to the inner pot of your Instant Pot. Put on the lid and set the vent to sealed. Cook on high pressure on Manual mode for 6 minutes.

2. Let the pressure release naturally.

3. Once pressure has completely released, remove lid, press the Cancel button to turn off the Instant Pot, then press the Sauté button and the adjust button until it sets to "less."

4. Add in the sauté ingredients. Mix well with a large spoon and mash the fruit pieces as you go.

5. Cook until it reaches the thickness you desire, then turn off and store in fridge once cooled.

Serving suggestion:

Great for an easy make-ahead side dish for a holiday meal!

Sangria Fruit

David Murphy

Makes 3 pints

1 bottle Moscato or Riesling

¼ cup brandy

⅓ cup Cointreau

1 kiwi peeled, halved, and sliced

1 orange, unpeeled and sliced thin

1 peach, wedged

1 plum, wedged

15 fresh figs, halved

½ cup red seedless grapes

½ cup green seedless grapes

1. Pour wine into your pot. Press Steam button at Normal setting. Allow wine to boil and be reduced by half. Press the Cancel button and allow to cool. Once cooled, add brandy and Cointreau.

2. Place fruit evenly into 3 pint-sized jars. Evenly distribute wine mixture among jars. Seal lids and allow to cool for 3 hours. Place in the fridge and allow to cool for 48 hours.

Cajun-Spiced Boiled Peanuts

David Murphy

Makes 1 pound

1 pound raw peanuts in the shell

¼ cup sea salt

1 teaspoon white distilled vinegar

7 cups water

1 tablespoon Slap Ya Mama or other Cajun seasoning

Note:

Please note that this cooking time will result in slightly firm peanuts. I don't like my boiled peanuts too soft. If you want southern-style "Slurpee" peanuts, then add an additional 45 to 50 minutes on the manual timer and let pressure naturally release.

1. Place all ingredients into your Instant Pot and stir with a wooden spoon to mix the ingredients around in the pot.

2. Close lid, and set your Instant Pot on Manual at high pressure for 30 minutes, and then let pressure naturally release.

3. Make sure all steam is released, remove lid, and serve! I like mine warm and not too hot.

Candied Pecans

Hope Comerford

Makes 10 servings

4 cups raw pecans

⅔ cup maple syrup

1 tablespoon water + ½ cup

1 teaspoon vanilla extract

1 teaspoon cinnamon

¼ teaspoon nutmeg

⅛ teaspoon ground ginger

⅛ teaspoon sea salt

1. Place the raw pecans, maple syrup, 1 tablespoon water, vanilla, cinnamon, nutmeg, ground ginger, and sea salt into the inner pot of the Instant Pot.

2. Press the Sauté button on the Instant Pot and sauté the pecans and other ingredients until the pecans are soft.

3. Pour in the ½ cup water and secure the lid to the locked position. Set the vent to sealing.

4. Press Manual on high pressure and set the Instant Pot for 15 minutes.

5. Preheat the oven to 350°F.

6. When cooking time is up, turn off the Instant Pot, then do a quick release.

7. Spread the pecans onto a greased, lined baking sheet.

8. Bake the pecans for 5 minutes or less in the oven, checking on them frequently so they do not burn.

Insta Popcorn

Hope Comerford

Makes 5–6 servings

2 tablespoon coconut oil

½ cup popcorn kernels

¼ cup butter

Sea salt to taste

1. Set the Instant Pot to Sauté.

2. Melt the coconut oil in the inner pot, then add the popcorn kernels and stir.

3. Press Adjust to bring the temperature up to high.

4. When the corn starts popping, secure the lid on the Instant Pot.

5. When you no longer hear popping, turn off the Instant Pot, remove the lid, and pour the popcorn into a bowl.

6. Season the popcorn with sea salt and butter to your liking.

Ghee

David Murphy

Makes 1 pint

1 pound grass-fed unsalted butter

1. Place butter into pot and press Sauté button at Normal setting.

2. Once it starts bubbling (approximately 5 to 6 minutes), adjust to Low Sauté setting. You should see the milk solids separating. In about 18 to 20 minutes, you will see that the milk solids have turned to a light golden-brown color. You have to pay attention or you will burn it. You want the milk solids to have a beautiful brown color. That's how you know it's done.

3. Once you achieve the color, remove the metal pot so it doesn't continue to cook and burn. Press the Cancel button to stop the heat.

4. Allow to cool for a couple of minutes. Strain melted butter through cheesecloth. Allow to cool and set. Your ghee is done!

Soups, Stews & Chilis

Chicken Cheddar Broccoli Soup

Maria Shevlin

Makes 4–6 servings

1 pound raw chicken breast, thinly chopped/sliced

1 pound fresh broccoli, chopped

½ cup onion, chopped

2 cloves garlic, minced

1 cup shredded carrots

½ cup finely chopped celery

¼ cup finely chopped red bell pepper

3 cups chicken bone broth

½ teaspoon salt

¼ teaspoon black pepper

½ teaspoon garlic powder

1 teaspoon parsley flakes

Pinch red pepper flakes

2 cups heavy cream

8 ounces freshly shredded cheddar cheese

2 tablespoons Frank's RedHot Original Cayenne Pepper Sauce

1. Place chicken, broccoli, chopped onion, garlic, carrots, celery, bell pepper, chicken broth, and seasonings in the pot and stir to mix.

2. Secure the lid and make sure vent is at sealing. Place on Manual at high pressure for 15 minutes.

3. Manually release the pressure when cook time us up, remove lid, and stir in heavy cream.

4. Place pot on sauté setting until it all comes to a low boil, approximately 5 minutes.

5. Stir in cheese and the hot sauce.

6. Turn off the pot as soon as you add the cheese and give it a stir.

7. Continue to stir until the cheese is melted.

Serving suggestion:

Serve it up with slice or two of keto garlic bread or bread of your choice.

Creamy Chicken Wild Rice Soup

Vonnie Oyer

Makes 4–6 servings

2 tablespoons butter

½ cup yellow onion, diced

¾ cup carrots, diced

¾ cup sliced mushrooms (about 3–4 mushrooms)

½ pound chicken breast, diced into 1-inch cubes

1 (6.2-oz.) box Uncle Ben's Long Grain & Wild Rice Fast Cook

2 (14-oz.) cans chicken broth

1 cup milk

1 cup half-and-half

2 ounces cream cheese

2 tablespoons cornstarch

1. Select the Sauté feature and add the butter, onion, carrots, and mushrooms to the inner pot. Sauté for about 5 minutes until onions are translucent and soft.

2. Add the cubed chicken and seasoning packet from the Uncle Ben's box and stir to combine.

3. Add the wild rice and chicken broth. Select Manual, high pressure, then lock the lid and make sure the vent is set to sealing. Set the time for 5 minutes.

4. After the cooking time ends, allow it to stay on the keep warm setting for 5 minutes and then quick release the pressure.

5. Remove the lid; change the setting to the Sauté function again.

6. Add the milk, half-and-half, and cream cheese. Stir to melt.

7. In a small bowl, mix the cornstarch with a little bit of water to dissolve, then add to the soup to thicken.

Chicken Rice Soup

Karen Ceneviva

Makes 8 servings

1 teaspoon vegetable oil

2 ribs celery, chopped in ½-inch-thick pieces

1 medium onion, chopped

1 cup wild rice, uncooked

½ cup long-grain rice, uncooked

1 pound boneless skinless chicken breasts, cut into ¾-inch cubes

5¼ cups fat-free, low-sodium chicken broth

2 teaspoons dried thyme leaves

¼ teaspoon red pepper flakes

1. Using the Sauté function on the Instant Pot, heat the teaspoon of vegetable oil. Sauté the celery and onion until the onions are slightly translucent (3–5 minutes). Once cooked, press Cancel.

2. Add the remaining ingredients to the inner pot.

3. Secure the lid and make sure the vent is set to sealing. Using the Manual function, set the time to 10 minutes on high presure.

4. When cook time is over, let the pressure release naturally for 10 minutes, then perform a quick release.

Serving suggestion:

A dollop of fat-free sour cream sprinkled with finely chopped scallions on top of each individual serving bowl makes a nice finishing touch.

Chicken Vegetable Soup

Maria Shevlin

Makes 6 servings

1–2 raw chicken breasts, cubed

½ medium onion, chopped

4 cloves garlic, minced

½ sweet potato, cut into small cubes

1 large carrot, peeled and cubed

4 stalks celery, chopped, leaves included

½ cup frozen corn

¼ cup frozen peas

¼ cup frozen lima beans

1 cup frozen green beans, bite-size pieces

¼–½ cup chopped savoy cabbage

1 (14½-oz.) can petite diced tomatoes

3 cups chicken bone broth

1 teaspoon salt

½ teaspoon black pepper

1 teaspoon garlic powder

¼ cup chopped fresh parsley

¼–½ teaspoon red pepper flakes

1. Add all of the ingredients, in the order listed, to the inner pot of the Instant Pot.

2. Lock the lid in place, set the vent to sealing, press Manual, and cook at high pressure for 4 minutes.

3. Release the pressure manually as soon as cooking time is finished.

Chicken Noodle Soup

Colleen Heatwole

Makes 6–8 servings

2 tablespoons butter

1 tablespoon oil

1 medium onion, diced

2 large carrots, diced

3 ribs celery, diced

3 cloves garlic, minced

1 teaspoon thyme

1 teaspoon oregano

1 teaspoon basil

8 cups chicken broth

2 cups cubed cooked chicken

8 ounces medium egg noodles

1 cup frozen peas (thaw while preparing soup)

Salt to taste

Pepper to taste

1. In the inner pot of the Instant Pot, melt the butter with oil on the Sauté function.

2. Add onion, carrots, and celery with large pinch of salt and continue cooking on sauté until soft, about 5 minutes, stirring frequently.

3. Add garlic, thyme, oregano, and basil and sauté an additional minute.

4. Add broth, cooked chicken, and noodles, stirring to combine all ingredients.

5. Put lid on the Instant Pot and set vent to sealing. Select Manual high pressure and add 4 minutes.

6. When time is up do a quick (manual) release of the pressure.

7. Add thawed peas, stir, adjust seasoning with salt and pepper, and serve.

Asian Chicken Noodle Soup

Carol Eveleth

Makes 4–6 servings

6 cups cooked chicken, cubed

1 medium onion, chopped

3 stalks celery, sliced

1 bay leaf

6 cups chicken broth

2 medium carrots, thinly sliced

1 medium red bell pepper, coarsely chopped

8 ounces rice noodles

4 cloves garlic, minced

2 tablespoons reduced sodium soy sauce

2 tablespoons finely chopped fresh ginger

½ teaspoon sage

½ teaspoon black pepper

3 cups shredded cabbage

3–4 tablespoons rice vinegar

1. Put all ingredients into the inner pot of the Instant Pot.

2. Secure the lid on the pot. Close the pressure-release valve. Select Manual and cook at high pressure for 10 minutes.

3. When cooking is complete, use a quick release to depressurize. Press Cancel to turn the pot off.

Chicken Tortellini Soup

Bryan Woolley

Makes 4 servings

6–8 cups chicken stock

1 onion, chopped

5 carrots, sliced

5 celery stalks, sliced

2 cups chopped kale

3 cups frozen green beans

4 cups chicken tortellini, prepared per package instructions

1. Pour chicken stock into Instant Pot. Add chopped onion, carrots, celery, kale, and green beans.

2. Secure lid and set Instant Pot to pressure cook on high for 3 minutes. Let pressure release naturally.

3. Remove lid and add the prepared chicken tortellini.

4. Place lid back on Instant Pot. Pressure cook on high for an additional 3 minutes. Quick release the pressure. You may want to put a clean dish towel over the vent to prevent any liquid from splashing.

Serving suggestion:

I like to serve this soup with freshly baked Quick and Easy Cinnamon Rolls (page 12).

Unstuffed Cabbage Soup

Colleen Heatwole

Makes 4–6 servings

2 tablespoons coconut oil

1 pound ground beef, turkey, or venison

1 medium onion, diced

2 cloves garlic, minced

1 small head cabbage, chopped, cored, cut into roughly 2-inch pieces

1 (6-oz.) can tomato paste

1 (32-oz.) can diced tomatoes, with liquid

2 cups beef broth

1½ cups water

¾ cup white or brown rice

1–2 teaspoons salt

½ teaspoon black pepper

1 teaspoon oregano

1 teaspoon parsley

1. Melt coconut oil in the inner pot of the Instant Pot using Sauté function. Add ground meat. Stir frequently until meat loses color, about 2 minutes.

2. Add onion and garlic and continue to sauté for 2 more minutes, stirring frequently.

3. Add chopped cabbage.

4. On top of cabbage layer tomato paste, tomatoes with liquid, beef broth, water, rice, and spices.

5. Secure the lid and set vent to sealing. Using Manual setting on high pressure, select 10 minutes if using white rice, 20 minutes if using brown rice.

6. When time is up, let the pressure release naturally for 10 minutes, then do a quick release.

Meatball and Pasta Soup

Michele Ruvola

Makes 4–5 servings

1 cup diced carrots

½ cup diced celery

¾ cup diced onion

20–25 mini meatballs, frozen

1½ cups ditalini pasta

40 ounces beef broth

1 teaspoon salt

½ teaspoon black pepper

2 tablespoons diced parsley

2 tablespoons diced green onions

1. Place all ingredients except parsley and green onions in the inner pot of the Instant Pot and stir.

2. Secure the lid, make sure vent is set to sealing, then put on Manual function, set to high pressure, for 9 minutes.

3. Use quick release to release pressure, then stir.

4. Top with parsley and green onions.

Split Pea Soup

Judy Gascho

Makes 3–4 servings

4 cups chicken broth

4 sprigs thyme

4 ounces ham, diced (about ⅓ cup)

2 tablespoons butter

2 stalks celery

2 carrots

1 large leek

3 cloves garlic

1½ cups dried green split peas (about 12 ounces)

1 cup water, optional

Salt to taste

Pepper to taste

1. Pour the broth into the inner pot of the Instant Pot and set to Sauté. Add the thyme, ham, and butter.

2. While the broth heats, chop the celery and cut the carrots into ½-inch-thick rounds. Halve the leek lengthwise and thinly slice and chop the garlic. Add the vegetables to the pot as you cut them. Rinse the split peas in a colander, discarding any small stones, then add to the pot.

3. Secure the lid, making sure the steam valve is in the sealing position. Set the cooker to Manual at high pressure for 15 minutes. When the time is up, carefully turn the steam valve to the venting position to release the pressure manually.

4. Turn off the Instant Pot. Remove the lid and stir the soup; discard the thyme sprigs.

5. Thin the soup with up to 1 cup water if needed (the soup will continue to thicken as it cools). Season with salt and pepper.

Split Pea Soup with Chicken Sausage

Colleen Heatwole

Makes 4–6 servings

1 pound ground chicken sausage

2 tablespoons oil

1 medium onion, finely chopped

1 medium carrot, peeled and diced

1 stalk celery, diced

2 cloves garlic, minced

32 ounces chicken stock

2 cups water

1 (16-oz.) package split peas, sorted and rinsed

¼ teaspoon dry red pepper flakes

½ cup half-and-half or whole milk

Salt to taste

Fresh ground pepper to taste

1. Using Sauté function, brown sausage in the inner pot of the Instant Pot. Remove to platter or bowl.

2. Heat the oil in the inner pot of the Instant Pot using Sauté function.

3. Sauté onion, carrot, and celery until tender, about 5 minutes.

4. Add garlic and sauté additional minute.

5. Add chicken stock, water, split peas, and red pepper flakes.

6. Secure lid and make sure vent is pointing to sealing. Using Manual mode, select 10 minutes cook time, high pressure.

7. When cook time is up, let the pressure release naturally for 10 minutes, then release the rest of the pressure manually.

8. Using immersion blender or food processor, puree the contents of the inner pot until mixture is very smooth.

9. Select Sauté and add sausage and half-and-half; heat until sausage is heated through.

10. Add salt and pepper to taste.

Potato Bacon Soup

Colleen Heatwole

Makes 4–6 servings

5 pounds potatoes, peeled and cubed

3 stalks celery, diced into roughly ¼- to ½-inch pieces

1 large onion, chopped

1 clove garlic, minced

1 tablespoon seasoning salt

½ teaspoon black pepper

4 cups chicken broth

1 pound bacon, fried crisp and rough chopped

1 cup half-and-half

1 cup milk, 2% or whole

Sour cream, shredded cheddar cheese, and diced green onion to garnish, optional

1. Place potatoes in bottom of the Instant Pot inner pot.

2. Add celery, onion, garlic, seasoning salt, and pepper, then stir to combine.

3. Add chicken broth and bacon to pot and stir to combine.

4. Secure the lid and make sure vent is in the sealing position. Using Manual mode select 5 minutes, high pressure.

5. Manually release the pressure when cooking time is up. Open pot and roughly mash potatoes, leaving some large chunks if desired.

6. Add half-and-half and milk.

7. Serve while still hot with desired assortment of garnishes.

Potato Soup

Michele Ruvola

Makes 4 servings

5 pounds russet potatoes, peeled and cubed

3 stalks celery, sliced thin

1 large onion, diced

1 clove garlic, minced

1 tablespoon seasoning salt

1 teaspoon ground black pepper

¼ cup butter

1 pound bacon, fried crisp, rough chopped

4 cups chicken stock

1 cup heavy cream

½ cup whole milk

Sour cream, shredded cheddar cheese, sliced green onions to garnish, optional

1. Put potatoes, celery, onion, garlic, seasoning salt, pepper and butter in the inner pot of the Instant Pot. Stir to combine.

2. Add bacon and chicken stock, then stir to combine.

3. Secure the lid and make sure the vent is on sealing. Push the Manual mode button, then set timer for 5 minutes on high pressure.

4. Quick release the steam when cook time is up.

5. Remove lid; mash potatoes to make a semi-smooth soup.

6. Add cream and milk; stir to combine.

7. Serve with garnishes if desired.

Serving suggestion:

Perfect on a cold night with slices of bread on the side or with a salad.

Potato and Corn Chowder

Janie Steele

Makes 4–6 servings

3 tablespoons butter

¼ cup diced onion

6 medium red potatoes, diced

4 ears corn, or frozen or canned (equal to 2 cups)

3 cups vegetable broth or water

2 teaspoons cornstarch

3 cups half-and-half

Grated cheddar cheese, optional

1. Place the butter in the inner pot of the Instant Pot. Press the Sauté function and let the butter melt.

2. Sauté the onion in the butter until translucent.

3. Add the potatoes, corn, and broth or water to the Inner Pot.

4. Secure the lid and set vent to sealing, then cook on Manual, high pressure, for 10 minutes.

5. Let the pressure release naturally, then remove lid.

6. Mix cornstarch in small amount of water and mix into soup to thicken.

7. With Instant Pot on sauté, add the half-and-half slowly while stirring.

8. Serve with cheddar cheese on top, if desired.

Ham and Potato Chowder

Penny Blosser

Makes 5 servings

1 (5-oz.) package scalloped potatoes

Sauce mix from potato package

1 cup extra-lean, reduced-sodium, cooked ham, cut into narrow strips

4 teaspoons sodium-free bouillon powder

4 cups water

1 cup chopped celery

⅓ cup chopped onions

Pepper to taste

2 cups fat-free half-and-half

⅓ cup flour

1. Combine potatoes, sauce mix, ham, bouillon powder, water, celery, onions, and pepper in the inner pot of the Instant Pot.

2. Secure the lid and cook using the Slow Cook function on low for 7 hours.

3. Combine half-and-half and flour. Remove the lid and gradually add to the inner pot, blending well.

4. Secure the lid once more and cook on the low Slow Cook function for up to 1 hour more, stirring occasionally until thickened.

Bacon and Corn Chowder

Bryan Woolley

Makes 6 servings

½ pound bacon, chopped

1 medium onion, chopped

3 medium potatoes, peeled and diced into ½-inch cubes

4–5 stalks celery, chopped

3–4 carrots, peeled and chopped

3 cups corn

1 tablespoon paprika

2 tablespoons flour

2 cups milk

3 cups chicken stock

Salt to taste

Freshly cracked pepper to taste

½ cup freshly chopped parsley to garnish

1. Set Instant Pot on Sauté mode and allow to heat up.

2. Add bacon and sauté for 2 to 3 minutes.

3. Add chopped onion and diced potatoes and sauté for another 2 to 3 minutes.

4. Add chopped celery, carrots, corn, and paprika to the bacon. Sauté for another minute.

5. Sprinkle bacon and vegetables with flour and stir to incorporate.

6. Once flour is incorporated, pour milk and chicken stock into pot. Stir to incorporate everything.

7. Secure the Instant Pot lid. Set the pressure cooker on low for 10 minutes. Let pressure release naturally.

8. Once pressure has released, remove lid, adjust salt and pepper to taste. Sprinkle with chopped parsley to garnish.

Butternut Squash Soup

Colleen Heatwole

Makes 4 servings

2 tablespoons butter

1 large onion, chopped

2 cloves garlic, minced

1 teaspoon thyme

½ teaspoon sage

Salt to taste

Pepper to taste

2 large butternut squash, peeled, seeded, and cubed (about 4 pounds)

4 cups chicken stock

1. In the inner pot of the Instant Pot, melt the butter using sauté function.

2. Add onion and garlic and cook until soft, 3 to 5 minutes.

3. Add thyme and sage and cook another minute. Season with salt and pepper.

4. Stir in butternut squash and add chicken stock.

5. Secure the lid and make sure vent is at sealing. Using Manual setting, cook squash and seasonings 10 minutes, using high pressure.

6. When time is up, do a quick release of the pressure.

7. Puree the soup in a food processor or use immersion blender right in the inner pot. If soup is too thick, add more stock. Adjust salt and pepper as needed.

Brown Lentil Soup

Colleen Heatwole

Makes 3–5 servings

1 medium onion, chopped

1 tablespoon olive oil

1 medium carrot, diced

2 cloves garlic, minced

1 small bay leaf

1 pound brown lentils

5 cups chicken broth

1 teaspoon salt

¼ teaspoon ground black pepper

½ teaspoon lemon juice

1. Using the Sauté function, sauté the chopped onion in oil in the inner pot of the Instant Pot about 2 minutes, or until it starts to soften.

2. Add diced carrot and sauté 3 minutes more until it begins to soften. Stir frequently or it will stick.

3. Add garlic and sauté 1 more minute.

4. Add bay leaf, lentils, and broth to pot.

5. Secure the lid and make sure vent is at sealing. Using Manual setting, select 14 minutes and cook on high pressure.

6. When cooking time is up, do a quick release of the pressure.

7. Discard bay leaf.

8. Stir in salt, pepper, and lemon juice, then adjust seasonings to taste.

Black Bean Soup

Colleen Heatwole

Makes 4–6 servings

2 tablespoons coconut oil

1 cup coarsely chopped onion

2 cups dry black beans, cleaned of debris and rinsed

6 cups vegetable or chicken broth

3 cloves garlic, minced

½ teaspoon paprika

⅛ teaspoon red pepper flakes

2 large bay leaves

1 teaspoon cumin

2 teaspoons oregano

½ teaspoon salt (or more if desired)

Yogurt and sour cream to garnish, optional

1. Heat the oil in the inner pot of the Instant Pot with the sauté function. Add onion and sauté 2 minutes.

2. Add remaining ingredients except garnishes, and stir well.

3. Secure lid and make sure vent is at sealing, then set to Bean/Chili for 25 minutes on high pressure.

4. After time is up let pressure release naturally.

5. Remove bay leaves and serve with desired garnishes.

Southwestern Bean Soup with Corn Dumplings

Melba Eshleman

Makes 8 servings

1 (15½-oz.) can red kidney beans, rinsed and drained

1 (15½-oz.) can black beans, pinto beans, or great northern beans, rinsed and drained

3 cups water

1 (14½-oz.) can Mexican-style stewed tomatoes

1 (10-oz.) package frozen whole-kernel corn, thawed

1 cup sliced carrots

1 cup chopped onions

1 (4-oz.) can chopped green chilies

3 teaspoons sodium-free instant bouillon powder, any flavor

1–2 teaspoons chili powder

2 cloves garlic, minced

Dumplings

⅓ cup flour

¼ cup yellow cornmeal

1 teaspoon baking powder

Dash pepper

1 egg white, beaten

2 tablespoons milk

1 tablespoon oil

1. Combine the 11 soup ingredients in inner pot of the Instant Pot.

2. Secure the lid and cook on the Low Slow Cook setting for 10 to 12 hours or high for 4 to 5 hours.

3. Make dumplings by mixing together flour, cornmeal, baking powder, and pepper.

4. Combine egg white, milk, and oil. Add to flour mixture. Stir with fork until just combined.

5. At the end of the soup's cooking time, turn the Instant Pot to Slow Cook function high if you don't already have it there. Remove the lid and drop dumpling mixture by rounded teaspoonfuls to make 8 mounds atop the soup.

6. Secure the lid once more and cook for an additional 30 minutes.

Great Northern Bean and Klondike Rose Potato Soup

Bryan Woolley

Makes 6–8 servings

1½ cups dry great northern beans

8 cups water

8 cups chicken stock

2 cups chopped kale

2 tablespoons Italian herb blend

4 medium Klondike Rose potatoes, cut into pieces

2 tablespoons tomato paste

1 tablespoon olive oil

2 cups chopped onions

1 cup chopped carrot

1 cup chopped celery

2 cloves garlic, minced

Salt to taste

Pepper to taste

4 cups spinach

1. Rinse great northern beans, checking to make sure there are no small stones.

2. Place beans inside Instant Pot. Add 8 cups water and let the beans rehydrate for 30 minutes.

3. Strain water off beans and pour chicken stock over them. Secure lid. Pressure cook on high for 20 minutes. Allow steam to release naturally.

4. Remove lid and add remaining ingredients except spinach. Secure Instant Pot lid. Pressure cook on low for 5 minutes. Allow steam to release naturally.

5. Remove lid and stir in spinach. Let soup sit for 10 minutes before serving.

Ground Turkey Stew

Carol Eveleth

Makes 4–6 servings

1 tablespoon oil

1 onion, chopped

1 pound ground turkey

½ teaspoon garlic powder

1 teaspoon chili powder

¾ teaspoon cumin

2 teaspoons coriander

1 teaspoon dried oregano

½ teaspoon salt

1 green pepper, chopped

1 red pepper, chopped

1 tomato, chopped

1½ cups tomato sauce

1 tablespoon soy sauce

1 cup water

2 handfuls cilantro, chopped

1 (15-oz.) can black beans

1. Press the Sauté function on the control panel of the Instant Pot.

2. Add the oil to the inner pot and let it get hot. Add onion, season with salt, and sauté for a few minutes, or until light golden.

3. Add ground turkey. Break the ground meat using a wooden spoon to avoid formation of lumps. Sauté for a few minutes, until the pink color has faded.

4. Add garlic powder, chili powder, cumin, coriander, dried oregano, and salt. Combine well. Add green pepper, red pepper, and chopped tomato. Combine well.

5. Add tomato sauce, soy sauce, and water; combine well.

6. Close and secure the lid. Click on the Cancel key to cancel the Sauté mode. Make sure the pressure release valve on the lid is in the sealing position.

7. Click on Manual function first and then select high pressure. Click the + button and set the time to 15 minutes.

(Continued on next page)

8. You can either have the steam release naturally (it will take around 20 minutes) or, after 10 minutes, turn the pressure release valve on the lid to venting and release steam. Be careful as the steam is very hot. After the pressure has released completely, open the lid.

9. If the stew is watery, turn on the Sauté function and let it cook for a few more minutes with the lid off.

10. Add cilantro and can of black beans, combine well, and let cook for a few minutes.

Serving suggestion:

You can serve this with pasta—add pasta into a bowl and add cheddar cheese on top.

Beef Stew

Carol Eveleth

Makes 6 servings

2 pounds chuck steak,
1½-inch thickness

2 teaspoons salt (or to taste)

½ teaspoon black pepper

1 tablespoon Worcestershire
sauce

1 tablespoon light soy sauce

3 tablespoons tomato paste

1½ cups low-sodium chicken
stock

12 white mushrooms, thinly
sliced

2 small onions, thinly sliced

3 cloves garlic, crushed and
minced

2 celery stalks, cut into
1½-inch chunks

2 carrots, cut into 1½-inch
chunks

¼ cup apple juice

2 bay leaves

¼ teaspoon dried thyme

3–4 small Yukon gold
potatoes, quartered

1 tablespoon flour

½ cup frozen peas

1. Heat up your Instant Pot by pressing the Sauté button and click the adjust button to go to Sauté More function. Wait until the indicator says "hot."

2. Season one side of the chuck steak generously with salt and ground black pepper. Add olive oil into the inner pot. Be sure to coat the oil over whole bottom of the pot.

3. Carefully place the seasoned side of chuck steak in the inner pot. Generously season the other side with salt and ground black pepper. Brown for 6–8 minutes on each side without constantly flipping the steak. Remove and set aside in a large mixing bowl.

4. While the chuck steak is browning, mix together the Worcestershire sauce, light soy sauce, and tomato paste with the chicken stock.

5. Add sliced mushrooms into the Instant Pot. Sauté until all moisture from the mushrooms has evaporated and the edges are slightly crisped and browned, about 6 minutes. Taste and season with salt and ground black pepper if necessary. Remove and set aside.

(Continued on next page)

6. Add olive oil into Instant Pot if necessary. Add thinly sliced small onions and sauté until softened and slightly browned. Add minced garlic cloves and stir for roughly 30 seconds until fragrant.

7. Add all celery and carrots and sauté until slightly browned. Season with salt and freshly ground black pepper if necessary.

8. Pour in apple juice and completely deglaze bottom of the pot by scrubbing the flavorful brown bits with a wooden spoon.

9. Add 2 bay leaves, dried thyme, quartered potatoes, and chicken stock mixture in the pot. Mix well. Close and secure lid and pressure cook on Manual at high pressure for 4 minutes. When time is up, quick release the pressure. Open the lid.

10. While the vegetables are pressure cooking, cut the chuck steak into 1½- to 2-inch stew cubes on a large chopping board.

11. Place all chuck stew meat and the flavorful meat juice back in the large mixing bowl. Add flour in mixing bowl and mix well with the stew meat.

12. Remove half of the carrots, celery, and potatoes from pressure cooker and set aside. Place beef stew meat and all its juice in the inner pot. Partially submerge the beef stew meat in the liquid without stirring, as you don't want too much flour in the liquid at this point.

13. Close and secure the lid and pressure cook on Manual at high pressure for 32 minutes. When time is up, turn off the Instant Pot and quick release any remaining pressure.

14. On medium heat by pressing the Sauté button, break down the mushy potatoes and carrots with a wooden spoon. Stir to thicken the stew.

15. Add frozen peas, sautéed mushrooms, and the set-aside carrots, celery, and potatoes in the pot. Taste and season with salt and ground black pepper if necessary.

16. Serve with mashed potatoes, pasta, or your favorite starch. Enjoy!

Beef and Kale Stew

Dora Martindale

Makes 6 servings

1 cup sliced mushrooms

3 tablespoons butter

2 pounds ground beef

4 pieces nitrate-free bacon, chopped

2 bundles kale, finely chopped

4 cloves garlic, minced

2 onions, chopped

3–4 cups homemade beef bone broth, divided

3 large potatoes, chopped

3 teaspoons salt (or more to taste)

1 teaspoon pepper (or more to taste)

2 tablespoons dried thyme (or 2 drops Young Living Thyme Vitality Essential Oil)

2 heaping teaspoons non-GMO organic cornstarch

1. In the inner pot of the Instant Pot, sauté mushrooms in the butter using the Sauté function, then place in a bowl.

2. Add the beef, chopped bacon, kale, garlic, and onions, and sauté until beef is brown and kale is reduced in size.

3. Add 2 cups bone broth, thyme, salt, and pepper. Secure the lid and make sure vent is at sealing, then cook on Manual at high pressure for 8 minutes.

4. Do a quick release of the pressure.

5. Add the rest of ingredients (except the cornstarch) and 1 to 2 more cups of bone broth.

6. Secure the lid and make sure vent is at sealing, then cook on Manual at high pressure 6 minutes. Let the pressure release naturally.

7. Thicken slightly with the cornstarch and add more salt or pepper as needed.

Easy Southern Brunswick Stew

Barbara Sparks

Makes 12 servings

2 pounds pork butt, visible fat removed

1 (17-oz.) can white corn

1¼ cups ketchup

2 cups diced, cooked potatoes

1 (10-oz.) package frozen peas

2 (10¾-oz.) cans reduced-sodium tomato soup

Hot sauce to taste, optional

1. Place pork in the Instant Pot and secure the lid.

2. Press the Slow Cook setting and cook on low 6 to 8 hours.

3. When cook time is over, remove the meat from the bone and shred, removing and discarding all visible fat.

4. Combine all the meat and remaining ingredients (except the hot sauce) in the inner pot of the Instant Pot.

5. Secure the lid once more and cook in Slow Cook mode on low for 30 minutes more. Add hot sauce if you wish.

Tuscan Beef Stew

Karen Ceneviva

Makes 8 servings

1 (10½-oz.) can tomato soup

1 (10½-oz.) can fat-free, low-sodium beef broth

½ cup water

1 teaspoon Italian seasoning

½ teaspoon garlic powder

1 (14½-oz.) can Italian diced tomatoes

¾ pound carrot chunks, cut into 1-inch pieces

2 pounds stewing beef, cut into 1-inch cubes

2 (15½-oz.) cans cannellini beans, rinsed and drained

1. Mix all ingredients except beans in the inner pot of the Instant Pot.

2. Secure the lid and set the Instant Pot to the Slow Cook mode on high for 4 to 5 hours, or on low 8 to 9 hours, or until vegetables and beef are tender.

3. Remove the lid, add in the beans, and cook on Slow Cook mode once more, high for 10 more minutes.

Instantly Good Beef Stew

Hope Comerford

Makes 6 servings

3 tablespoons olive oil, divided

2 pounds stewing beef, cubed

2 cloves garlic, minced

1 large onion, chopped

3 ribs celery, sliced

3 large potatoes, cubed

2–3 carrots, sliced

8 ounces no-salt-added tomato sauce

10 ounces low-sodium beef broth

2 teaspoons Worcestershire sauce

¼ teaspoon pepper

1 bay leaf

1. Set the Instant Pot to the Sauté function, then add in 1 tablespoon of the oil. Add in ⅓ of the beef cubes and brown and sear all sides. Repeat this process twice more with the remaining oil and beef cubes. Set the beef aside.

2. Place the garlic, onion, and celery into the pot and sauté for a few minutes. Press Cancel.

3. Add the beef back in as well as all of the remaining ingredients.

4. Secure the lid and make sure the vent is set to sealing. Choose Manual for 35 minutes on high pressure.

5. When cook time is up, let the pressure release naturally for 15 minutes, then release any remaining pressure manually.

6. Remove the lid, remove the bay leaf, then serve.

Beef Dumpling Soup

Barbara Walker

Makes 6 servings

1 pound beef stewing meat, trimmed of visible fat, cubed

1 recipe onion soup mix, dry, salt-free

6 cups water

2 carrots, shredded

1 celery rib, finely chopped

1 tomato, peeled and chopped

2 cloves garlic

½ teaspoon dried basil

¼ teaspoon dill weed

1 cup buttermilk biscuit mix

1 tablespoon finely chopped parsley

6 tablespoons fat-free milk

1. Place meat in inner pot of the Instant Pot. Sprinkle with onion soup mix. Pour water over meat.

2. Add carrots, celery, tomato, garlic, basil and dill weed.

3. Secure the lid, or cover with the glass lid. Cook on the Slow Cook setting, Low, for 6 hours, or until meat is tender.

4. Combine biscuit mix and parsley. Stir in milk with fork until moistened. Drop dumplings by teaspoonfuls into pot.

5. Secure the lid once more, then cook on high Slow Cook mode for 30 minutes more.

Nancy's Vegetable Beef Soup

Nancy Graves

Makes 8 servings

1 (2-lb.) roast, cubed (or 2 pounds stewing meat)

1 (15-oz.) can corn

1 (15-oz.) can green beans

1 (1-lb.) bag frozen peas

1 (40-oz.) can no-added-salt stewed tomatoes

5 teaspoons salt-free beef bouillon powder

Tabasco to taste

½ teaspoon salt

Water to fill pot

1. Combine all ingredients in the Instant Pot except the water. Do not drain vegetables.

2. Add water to fill inner pot only to the fill line.

3. Secure the lid, or use the glass lid and set the Instant Pot on Slow Cook mode, Low for 8 hours, or until meat is tender and vegetables are soft.

White Chicken Chili

Judy Gascho

Makes 6 servings

2 tablespoons cooking oil

1½–2 pounds boneless chicken breasts or thighs

1 medium onion, chopped

3 cloves garlic, minced

2 cups chicken broth

3 (15-oz.) cans great northern beans, undrained

1 (15-oz.) can white corn, drained

1 (4½-oz.) can chopped green chilies, undrained

1 teaspoon cumin

½ teaspoon ground oregano

1 cup sour cream

1½ cups grated cheddar or Mexican blend cheese

1. Set Instant Pot to Sauté and allow the inner pot to get hot.

2. Add oil and chicken. Brown chicken on both sides.

3. Add onions, garlic, chicken broth, undrained beans, drained corn, undrained green chilies, cumin, and oregano.

4. Place lid on and close valve to sealing.

5. Set to Bean/Chili for 30 minutes on high pressure.

6. Let pressure release naturally for 15 minutes before carefully releasing any remaining steam.

7. Remove chicken and shred.

8. Put chicken, sour cream, and cheese in the inner pot. Stir until cheese is melted.

Serving suggestion:

Can serve with chopped cilantro and additional cheese.

Favorite Chili

Carol Eveleth

Makes 4–6 servings

1 pound ground beef

1 teaspoon salt

½ teaspoon black pepper

1 tablespoon olive oil

1 small onion, chopped

2 cloves garlic, minced

1 green pepper, chopped

2 tablespoons chili powder

½ teaspoon cumin

1 cup water

1 (16-oz.) can chili beans

1 (15-oz.) can crushed tomatoes

1. Press Sauté button and adjust once to Sauté More function. Wait until indicator says "hot."

2. Season the ground beef with salt and black pepper.

3. Add the olive oil into the inner pot. Coat the whole bottom of the pot with the oil.

4. Add ground beef into the inner pot. The ground beef will start to release moisture. Allow the ground beef to brown and crisp slightly, stirring occasionally to break it up. Taste and adjust the seasoning with more salt and ground black pepper.

5. Add diced onion, minced garlic, chopped pepper, chili powder, and cumin. Sauté for about 5 minutes, until the spices start to release their fragrance. Stir frequently.

6. Add water and can of chili beans, not drained. Mix well. Pour in can of crushed tomatoes.

7. Close and secure lid, making sure vent is set to sealing, and pressure cook on Manual at high pressure for 10 minutes.

8. Let the pressure release naturally when cooking time is up. Open the lid carefully.

Turkey Chili

Reita F. Yoder

Makes 8 servings

2 pounds ground turkey

1 small onion, chopped

1 clove garlic, minced

1 (16-oz.) can low-sodium pinto or kidney beans

2 cups chopped fresh tomatoes

2 cups no-salt-added tomato sauce

1 (16-oz.) can Rotel tomatoes

1 (1-oz.) package low-sodium chili seasoning

1. Turn the Instant Pot to Sauté and add a touch of olive oil or cooking spray to the inner pot. Crumble ground turkey in the inner pot and brown on the Sauté setting until cooked. Add in onions and garlic and sauté an additional 5 minutes, stirring constantly.

2. Add remaining ingredients to inner pot and mix well.

3. Secure the lid and make sure the vent is set to sealing. Cook on Manual for 5 minutes on high pressure.

4. When cook time is up, let the pressure release naturally for 10 minutes, then manually release the rest.

Three-Bean Chili

Chris Kaczynski

Makes 6 servings

1 pound extra-lean ground beef

1 medium onion, diced

1 cup medium salsa

1 package low-sodium dry chili seasoning

1 (16-oz.) can low-sodium red kidney beans, drained

1 (16-oz.) can low-sodium black beans, drained

1 (16-oz.) can low-sodium white kidney, or garbanzo, beans drained

1 (14-oz.) can low-sodium crushed tomatoes

1 (14-oz.) can low-sodium diced tomatoes

5 drops liquid stevia

1. Turn the Instant Pot to Sauté and add a touch of olive oil or cooking spray to the inner pot. Brown the beef and onion. Press Cancel when done.

2. Stir in the remaining ingredients.

3. Secure the lid and make sure vent is set to sealing. Press Manual and set for 15 minutes on high pressure.

4. When cooking time is done, let the pressure release naturally for 10 minutes and then manually release the rest.

Vegetarian Chili

Connie Johnson

Makes 6 servings

2 teaspoons olive oil

3 cloves garlic, minced

2 onions, chopped

1 green bell pepper, chopped

1 cup textured vegetable protein (T.V.P.)

1-pound can beans of your choice, drained

1 jalapeño pepper, seeds removed, chopped

1 (28-oz.) can diced Italian tomatoes

1 bay leaf

1 tablespoon dried oregano

½ teaspoon salt

¼ teaspoons pepper

1. Set the Instant Pot to the Sauté function. As it's heating, add the olive oil, garlic, onions, and bell pepper. Stir constantly for about 5 minutes as it all cooks. Press Cancel.

2. Place all of the remaining ingredients into the inner pot of the Instant pot and stir.

3. Secure the lid and make sure vent is set to sealing. Cook on Manual mode for 10 minutes on high pressure.

4. When cook time is up, let the steam release naturally for 5 minutes and then manually release the rest.

French Market Soup

Ethel Mumaw

Makes 8 servings (about 2½ quarts total)

2 cups mixed dry beans, washed, with stones removed

7 cups water

1 ham hock, all visible fat removed

1 teaspoon salt

¼ teaspoon pepper

1 (16-oz.) can low-sodium tomatoes

1 large onion, chopped

1 clove garlic, minced

1 chile, chopped, or
   1 teaspoon chili powder

¼ cup lemon juice

1. Combine all ingredients in the inner pot of the Instant Pot.

2. Secure the lid and make sure vent is set to sealing. Using Manual, set the Instant Pot to cook for 60 minutes on high pressure.

3. When cooking time is over, let the pressure release naturally. When the Instant Pot is ready, unlock the lid, then remove the bone and any hard or fatty pieces. Pull the meat off the bone and chop into small pieces. Add the ham back into the Instant Pot.

French Onion Soup

Jenny R. Unternahrer, Janice Yoskovich

Makes 10 servings

½ cup light, soft tub margarine

8–10 large onions, sliced

3 (14-oz.) cans 98% fat-free, lower-sodium beef broth

2½ cups water

3 teaspoons sodium-free chicken bouillon powder

1½ teaspoons Worcestershire sauce

3 bay leaves

10 (1-oz.) slices French bread, toasted

1. Turn the Instant Pot to the Sauté function and add in the margarine and onions. Cook about 5 minutes, or until the onions are slightly soft. Press Cancel.

2. Add the beef broth, water, bouillon powder, Worcestershire sauce, and bay leaves and stir.

3. Secure the lid and make sure vent is set to sealing. Cook on Manual mode for 20 minutes on high pressure.

4. Let the pressure release naturally for 15 minutes, then do a quick release. Open the lid and discard bay leaves.

5. Ladle into bowls. Top each with a slice of bread and some cheese if you desire.

Italian Vegetable Soup

Patti Boston

Makes 6 servings

3 small carrots, sliced

1 small onion, chopped

2 small potatoes, diced

2 tablespoons chopped parsley

1 clove garlic, minced

3 teaspoons sodium-free beef bouillon powder

1¼ teaspoons dried basil

¼ teaspoon pepper

1 (16-oz.) can red kidney beans, undrained

3 cups water

1 (14½-oz.) can stewed tomatoes, with juice

1 cup diced cooked ham, extra-lean, lower-sodium

1. In the inner pot of the Instant Pot, layer the carrots, onion, potatoes, parsley, garlic, beef bouillon, basil, pepper, and kidney beans. Do not stir. Add water.

2. Secure the lid and cook on the Low Slow Cook mode for 8 to 9 hours, or on high 4½ to 5½ hours, until vegetables are tender.

3. Remove the lid and stir in the tomatoes and ham. Secure the lid again and cook on high Slow Cook mode for 10 to 15 minutes more.

Garlic Tomato Soup

Bryan Woolley

Makes 6–8 servings

14 tomatoes, sliced in half

1 tablespoon minced garlic

1 large onion, chopped

2 bell peppers, chopped

6 cups chicken stock

2 cups heavy cream

2 cups chopped fresh basil leaves

Salt and freshly cracked pepper to taste

Extra-virgin olive oil to drizzle

1. Place tomatoes into the Instant Pot. Add garlic, onion, bell peppers and chicken stock. Secure Instant Pot lid. Pressure cook on high for 20 minutes.

2. Allow pressure to release naturally.

3. Once pressure has released, add heavy cream and basil.

4. Using an immersion blender, puree ingredients together. Add salt and pepper to taste.

5. Drizzle extra-virgin olive oil over each bowl of soup before serving.

Vegetable Detox Soup

David Murphy

Makes 8 servings

4 large carrots, peeled and sliced

½ head cabbage (or 2 cups pre-shredded coleslaw mix)

2 Vidalia sweet onions, diced

1 head garlic, peeled and chopped

2 cups green beans, fresh or frozen, cut into bite-size pieces

10 ounces fresh kale, tough stems removed and chopped

6 cups vegetable broth

12 ounces salsa

1 tablespoon chili powder

2 teaspoons dried oregano

2 teaspoons cumin

2 teaspoons paprika

Salt to taste

Pepper to taste

7 green onions, sliced

6 ounces fresh baby spinach leaves

1. Add all ingredients to your pot, except baby spinach and green onions. Lock lid and close vent. Cook for 6 minutes on Manual at high pressure. As you add in your kale, don't be afraid to push those ingredients down into the pot. Once your ingredients start cooking away, the kale and cabbage are going to release moisture and wilt. Just try to leave a divot around where the pressure pin is.

2. Once done, quick release any pressure. Remove lid, and add baby spinach and green onions. Stir until spinach has wilted into your soup. Serve away! Stores great in the freezer.

Miso Soup

David Murphy

Makes 4 servings

3 tablespoons olive oil

1 teaspoon minced garlic

1 tablespoon ginger, peeled and minced

4 ounces shiitake or maitake mushrooms, sliced thin

Sea salt to taste

Pepper to taste

1 cup chopped kale

4 cups miso broth

½ teaspoon chili flakes

1 pack extra-firm tofu, cut into 1-inch cubes

1. Press Sauté button at Normal setting. Once pot is hot, add olive oil, garlic, ginger, and mushrooms. Cook for 5 to 7 minutes, being sure to stir occasionally.

2. Press Cancel and allow pot to cool for 5 minutes.

3. Add all remaining ingredients to pot except the tofu. Press Manual at high pressure and cook for 5 minutes. Once done, quick pressure release all pressure. Remove lid, and add in tofu. The tofu will heat up in no time, and then it's ready to serve!

Mayan Lime Soup

Bryan Woolley

Makes 4–6 servings

3 chicken breasts

4 cups chicken stock

3 tablespoons frying oil

1 clove garlic, crushed

1 small onion, sliced

1 fresh red pepper, sliced

2 ripe red tomatoes, chopped

2 bay leaves

2 limes, juiced and zest removed

Garnish

½ pound corn tortilla thin strips, fried to a golden crispy texture

1 lime, thinly sliced

1. Place chicken breasts and chicken stock into Instant Pot. Pressure cook on high for 30 minutes. Let pressure release naturally.

2. When steam has released, remove lid and carefully shred chicken breasts. Add them back into stock.

3. Add oil, crushed garlic clove, onion, red pepper, tomatoes, bay leaves, and zest and juice from 2 limes. Pressure cook on low for 3 minutes. Let pressure release naturally.

4. Remove lid and the bay leaves and ladle soup into favorite soup bowls.

5. Garnish each with fried corn tortilla strips and a thin slice of lime.

Spicy Pork Ramen

Bryan Woolley

Makes 4 servings

1 cup dry kidney beans
6 cups cold water
Vegetable oil
1½ pounds country-style pork
  ribs
6 cups chicken stock
1 (16-oz.) can diced
  tomatoes, with juice
1 tablespoon hot chili sauce
3 carrots, chopped
2 onions, chopped
5–6 cloves garlic, peeled and
  minced
4 bay leaves
1 teaspoon dried oregano
2 cups corn
6 packages ramen noodles
Salt to taste
Pepper to taste

Garnish
1 bunch cilantro, chopped
1 bunch green onions chopped
1 Japanese fish cake
  (Narutomaki), sliced
2 cups diced extra firm tofu
3 hard-boiled eggs

1. Soak dry kidney beans in the cold water for 30 minutes. Drain water.

2. Select Sauté mode on Instant Pot. Add enough oil to lightly coat bottom of pan.

3. Add country-style pork ribs. Brown all sides.

4. Add chicken stock, tomatoes, chili sauce, kidney beans, carrots, onions, garlic, bay leaves, and oregano.

5. Pressure cook on high for 30 minutes. Allow steam to release naturally.

6. Remove lid. Make sure ribs shred easily and kidney beans are cooked. If not, pressure cook for 10 minutes longer, or adjust additional cooking time as needed. Allow pressure to release naturally.

7. Once cooked, select Sauté mode and add corn while bringing soup to a boil. Place ramen noodles in pot. Cook noodles for about 3 minutes or until tender. Add salt and pepper to taste.

8. Divide broth, pork, beans, and noodles between 4 large bowls, removing any bay leaves and garnishing with chopped cilantro, green onions, sliced fish cake, diced tofu, and hard-boiled eggs.

Ghormeh Sabzi

David Murphy

Makes 4 servings

1 tablespoon salted butter

1 large yellow onion, finely chopped

1½ pounds lamb or beef stew meat, cubed

4 bunches parsley, leaves only

1 bunch cilantro, leaves only

4 leeks, diced

1 tablespoon dried fenugreek (or 1 bunch fresh fenugreek)

4 dried black limes (limoo amani), or 4 tablespoons lemon juice

1 tablespoon turmeric

Sea salt

Cracked black pepper

1 cup water (I used hot water to help build pressure faster)

1 cup dark red kidney beans, drained

1. Turn your Instant Pot on Sauté mode. Add butter and yellow onion. Cook for approximately 2 minutes.

2. Add your meat, and then all remaining ingredients. Just be sure that the meat is on the bottom. I added the kidney beans last on top of all of the ingredients.

3. Lock your lid and close the vent. Place on Manual at high pressure for 15 minutes, then let pressure naturally release for about 18 to 20 minutes.

4. Once done, release any remaining pressure. Remove lid at an angle to ensure you're not dripping on yourself by accident. Give it a good stir before serving.

Quick Soupe de Poisson

David Murphy

Makes 4 servings

2 tablespoons olive oil

2 Vidalia sweet onions, roughly chopped

2 pounds mixed seafood (salmon, white fish, and whole prawns work best)

5 tomatoes, chopped

2 cloves garlic, minced

1 fennel bulb, chopped

2 bay leaves

1 long strip pared orange rind

3 sprigs thyme

1 tablespoon tomato paste

4 cups fish stock

2 cups lobster bisque

½ cup heavy cream

1. Turn your pot on in Normal Sauté mode and add oil. Once oil is heated, add onions, and cook, stirring often, until they start to soften.

2. Add seafood, tomatoes, garlic, and fennel, then stir for 2 minutes. Add bay leaves, orange rind, thyme, and tomato paste and stir to combine. Add the fish stock. Bring to a slight boil.

3. Once brought to a boil, press the Cancel button. Wait 5 minutes, and then lock the lid and close the vent. Cook on Manual on high pressure for 10 minutes and allow pressure to naturally release.

4. Strain contents through a sieve, pressing down on solids to extract all the flavor that you can.

5. Press Sauté button in Less Heat setting. Return stock to your pot and add lobster bisque and simmer. Cook for 10 to 15 minutes until slightly reduced.

6. Stir in cream, then simmer for 1 minute until heated through.

Poultry

Garlic Galore Rotisserie Chicken

Hope Comerford

Makes 4 servings

1 (3-lb.) whole chicken

2 tablespoons olive oil, divided

Salt to taste

Pepper to taste

20–30 cloves fresh garlic, peeled and left whole

1 cup chicken stock, broth, or water

2 tablespoons garlic powder

2 teaspoons onion powder

½ teaspoon basil

½ teaspoon cumin

½ teaspoon chili powder

1. Rub chicken with 1 tablespoon of olive oil and sprinkle with salt and pepper.

2. Place the garlic cloves inside the chicken. Use butcher's twine to secure the legs.

3. Press the Sauté button on the Instant Pot then add the rest of the olive oil to the inner pot.

4. When the pot is hot, place the chicken inside. You are just trying to sear it, so leave it for about 4 minutes on each side.

5. Remove the chicken and set aside. Place the trivet at the bottom of the inner pot and pour in the chicken stock.

6. Mix together the remaining seasonings and rub it all over the entire chicken.

7. Place the chicken back inside the inner pot, breast side up, on top of the trivet and secure the lid to the sealing position.

8. Press the Manual button and use the +/- to set it for 25 minutes on high pressure.

9. When the timer beeps, allow the pressure to release naturally for 15 minutes. If the lid will not open at this point, quick release the remaining pressure and remove the chicken.

10. Let the chicken rest for 5 to 10 minutes before serving.

Butter Chicken

Jessica Stoner

Makes 4 servings

1 tablespoon olive oil

1 medium onion, diced

1–2 medium cloves garlic, minced

½ tablespoon minced ginger

1 teaspoon garam masala

½ teaspoon turmeric

2 teaspoons kosher salt

2 pounds cubed boneless skinless chicken breast

¼ cup tomato paste

2 cups crushed tomatoes

½ cup water + more if needed

1½ tablespoons honey

1½ cups heavy cream

1 tablespoon butter

1. On Sauté function at high heat, heat oil in the inner pot of the Instant Pot. Add onion, garlic, and ginger and sauté for 1 minute, until fragrant and onion is soft.

2. Add garam masala, turmeric, and salt. Sauté quickly and add chicken. Stir to coat chicken. Add tomato paste and crushed tomatoes. Slowly add water, scraping the bottom of the pot with a spoon to make sure there are no bits of tomato stuck to the bottom. Stir in honey.

3. Secure the lid, making sure vent is turned to sealing function. Use the Poultry high pressure function and set cook time to 15 minutes. Once done cooking, do a quick release of the pressure.

4. Remove lid, change to medium/normal Sauté function, stir in heavy cream, and bring to a simmer. Simmer for 5 minutes, adding up to ¼ cup additional water if you need to thin the sauce out. Stir in butter until melted and turn off.

Serving suggestion:

Serve hot with basmati rice and naan bread.

Buttery Lemon Chicken

Judy Gascho

Makes 4 servings

2 tablespoons butter

1 medium onion, chopped

4 cloves garlic, minced

½ teaspoon paprika

½ teaspoon pepper

1 teaspoon dried parsley
(or 1 tablespoon chopped
fresh parsley)

2 pounds boneless chicken
breasts or thighs

½ cup chicken broth

⅓ cup lemon juice

1 teaspoon salt

1–2 tablespoons cornstarch

1. Set the Instant Pot to Sauté. When it is hot, add butter to the inner pot and melt.

2. Add the onion, garlic, paprika, pepper, and parsley to melted butter and sauté until onion starts to soften. Push onion to side of pot.

3. With the Instant Pot still at sauté, add the chicken and sear on each side 3–5 minutes.

4. Mix broth, lemon juice, and salt together. Pour over chicken and stir to mix all together.

5. Put on lid and set Instant Pot, move vent to sealing and press Poultry on high pressure. Set cook time for 7 minutes. Let depressurize naturally.

6. Remove chicken, leaving sauce in pot. Mix cornstarch in water and add to sauce. (Can start with 1 tablespoon cornstarch, and use second one if sauce isn't thick enough.)

Serving suggestion:

Serve chicken and sauce over noodles or rice.

Chicken with Lemon

Colleen Heatwole

Makes 4 servings

2 pounds boneless skinless chicken thighs

3 tablespoons olive oil, divided

1 teaspoon rosemary

1 teaspoon kosher salt

½ teaspoon black pepper

1 lemon, organic preferred

1 medium onion, diced

2 cloves garlic, minced

2 tablespoons water

1. Toss chicken with 1 tablespoon oil, rosemary, salt, and pepper.

2. Wash lemon, trim ends, quarter lengthwise, and remove seeds. Slice quarters crosswise into ⅛-inch slices.

3. Heat remaining 2 tablespoons oil in the inner pot using Sauté function of the Instant Pot.

4. Add onion and garlic and sauté 3 minutes, stirring frequently.

5. Add lemon and sauté an additional minute.

6. Add the water.

7. Add chicken and stir to combine.

8. Secure the lid and set vent to sealing. Cook 8 minutes, using Manual at high pressure.

9. Allow pressure to release naturally.

Slow Cooked Honey Garlic Chicken Thighs

Colleen Heatwole

Makes 2–4 servings

4 boneless skinless chicken thighs

2 tablespoons soy sauce

½ cup ketchup

⅓ cup honey

3 cloves garlic, minced

1 teaspoon basil

1. Place chicken thighs in bottom of the inner pot of the Instant Pot.

2. Whisk remaining ingredients together in bowl and pour over chicken.

3. Cook covered on the Slow Cook function on low pressure for 4 hours. Check for doneness. If not tender add additional time as needed.

Lemony Chicken Thighs

Maria Shevlin

Makes 3–5 servings

1 cup chicken bone broth

5 frozen bone-in chicken thighs

1 small onion, diced

5–6 cloves garlic, diced

Juice from 1 lemon

2 tablespoons butter, melted

½ teaspoon salt

¼ teaspoon black pepper

1 teaspoon True Lemon Lemon Pepper seasoning

1 teaspoon parsley flakes

¼ teaspoon oregano

Rind from 1 lemon

1. Add the chicken bone broth into the inner pot of the Instant Pot.

2. Add the chicken thighs.

3. Add the onion and garlic.

4. Pour the fresh lemon juice in with the melted butter.

5. Add the seasonings.

6. Lock the lid, make sure the vent is at sealing, then press the Poultry button. Set to 15 minutes on high pressure.

7. When cook time is up, let the pressure naturally release for 3 to 5 minutes, then manually release the rest.

8. You can place these under the broiler for 2 to 3 minutes to brown.

9. Plate up and pour some of the sauce over top with fresh grated lemon rind.

Orange Chicken Breasts

Anita Troyer

Makes 6 servings

2 pounds chicken breasts

2 tablespoons oil

Sauce

1 cup orange juice

1 tablespoon grated fresh ginger

4 cloves garlic, minced

1 tablespoon rice wine

½ cup tomato sauce

⅓ cup brown sugar

¼ cup soy sauce

Zest from 1 orange

2 tablespoons orange juice

2 tablespoons cornstarch

Serving suggestion:

Serve over rice.

1. Cut the chicken into 1- to 2-inch pieces.

2. Turn Instant Pot to Sauté. Once hot, add the oil to the inner pot. After the oil is hot, add the chicken and fry for 2 to 3 minutes, stirring several times. Make sure the chicken doesn't stick to the bottom of the pot.

3. Add the sauce ingredients to the chicken in the pot and stir to combine and coat chicken well.

4. Secure the lid on the pot and make sure vent is at sealing. Press the Manual function, at high pressure, for 5 minutes.

5. When cook time is up, turn off the Instant Pot and manually release the pressure.

6. Remove lid and turn pot on to Sauté.

7. Combine the orange juice and cornstarch in a small bowl and stir until well mixed. Add to pot and gently stir to combine. If stirred too vigorously, the chicken will fall apart.

8. Keep on Sauté setting until thickened, 2 to 3 minutes. Turn pot off.

Orange Chicken Thighs with Bell Peppers

Maria Shevlin

Makes 4–6 servings

6 boneless skinless chicken thighs, cut into bite-size pieces

2 packets crystallized True Orange flavoring

½ teaspoon True Orange Orange Ginger seasoning

½ teaspoon coconut aminos

¼ teaspoon Worcestershire sauce

Olive oil for the pot

2 cups bell pepper strips, any color combination (I used red, yellow, and orange)

1 onion, chopped

1 tablespoon green onion, chopped fine

3 cloves garlic, minced or chopped

½ teaspoon pink salt

½ teaspoon black pepper

1 teaspoon garlic powder

1 teaspoon ground ginger

¼–½ teaspoon red pepper flakes

2 tablespoons tomato paste

½ cup chicken bone broth or water

1 tablespoon brown sugar substitute (I use Sukrin Gold)

½ cup Seville orange spread (I use Crofter's brand)

1. Combine the chicken with the 2 packets of crystallized orange flavor, the orange ginger seasoning, the coconut aminos, and the Worcestershire sauce. Set aside.

2. Turn the Instant Pot to Sauté and add a touch of olive oil or cooking spray to the inner pot. Add in the orange ginger marinated chicken thighs.

(Continued on next page)

3. Sauté until lightly browned. Add in the peppers, onions, garlic, and seasonings. Mix well.

4. Add the remaining ingredients; mix to combine.

5. Lock the lid, set the vent to sealing, Press Manual and set to 7 minutes on high pressure.

6. Let the pressure release naturally for 2 minutes, then manually release the rest when cook time is up.

Serving suggestion:

Serve with your choice of pasta or rice and top with additional green onion and/or sesame seeds as well.

Chicken in Wine

Mary Seielstad

Makes 6 servings

2 pounds chicken breasts, trimmed of skin and fat

1 (10¾-oz.) can 98% fat-free, reduced-sodium cream of mushroom soup

1 (10¾-oz.) can French onion soup

1 cup dry white wine or chicken broth

1. Place the chicken into the Instant Pot.

2. Combine soups and wine. Pour over chicken.

3. Secure the lid and make sure vent is set to sealing. Cook on Manual mode for 12 minutes on high pressure.

4. When cook time is up, let the pressure release naturally for 5 minutes and then release the rest manually.

Greek Chicken

Judy Govotsos

Makes 6 servings

4 potatoes, unpeeled, quartered

2 pounds chicken pieces, trimmed of skin and fat

2 large onions, quartered

1 whole bulb garlic, cloves minced

3 teaspoons dried oregano

¾ teaspoon salt

½ teaspoon pepper

1 tablespoon olive oil

1 cup water

1. Place potatoes, chicken, onions, and garlic into the inner pot of the Instant Pot, then sprinkle with seasonings. Top with oil and water.

2. Secure the lid and make sure vent is set to sealing. Cook on Manual mode on high pressure for 20 minutes.

3. When cook time is over, let the pressure release naturally for 5 minutes, then release the rest manually.

Chicken Casablanca

Joyce Kaut

Makes 8 servings

2 large onions, sliced

1 teaspoon ground ginger

3 cloves garlic, minced

2 tablespoons canola oil, divided

3 pounds skinless chicken pieces

3 large carrots, diced

2 large potatoes, unpeeled, diced

½ teaspoon ground cumin

½ teaspoon salt

½ teaspoon pepper

¼ teaspoon cinnamon

2 tablespoons raisins

1 (14½-oz.) can chopped tomatoes

3 small zucchinis, sliced

1 (15-oz.) can garbanzo beans, drained

2 tablespoons chopped parsley

1. Using the Sauté function of the Instant Pot, cook the onions, ginger, and garlic in 1 tablespoon of oil for 5 minutes, stirring constantly. Remove onions, ginger, and garlic from pot and set aside.

2. Brown the chicken pieces with the remaining oil, then add the cooked onions, ginger and garlic back in as well as all of the remaining ingredients, except the parsley.

3. Secure the lid and make sure vent is in the sealing position. Cook on Manual mode on high pressure for 12 minutes.

4. When cook time is up, let the pressure release naturally for 5 minutes and then release the rest of the pressure manually.

Ann's Chicken Cacciatore

Ann Driscoll

Makes 8 servings

1 large onion, thinly sliced

3 pounds chicken, cut up, skin removed, trimmed of fat

2 (6-oz.) cans tomato paste

1 (4-oz.) can sliced mushrooms, drained

1 teaspoon salt

¼ cup dry white wine

¼ teaspoon pepper

1–2 cloves garlic, minced

1–2 teaspoons dried oregano

½ teaspoon dried basil

½ teaspoon celery seed, optional

1 bay leaf

1. In the inner pot of the Instant Pot, place the onion and chicken.

2. Combine remaining ingredients and pour over the chicken.

3. Secure the lid and make sure vent is at sealing. Cook on Slow Cook mode, low 7 to 9 hours, or high 3 to 4 hours.

Chicken Reuben Bake

Gail Bush

Makes 6 servings

4 boneless, skinless chicken-breast halves

¼ cup water

1 (1-lb.) bag sauerkraut, drained and rinsed

4–5 slices Swiss cheese (1 oz. each)

¾ cup fat-free Thousand Island salad dressing

2 tablespoons chopped fresh parsley

1. Place chicken and water in inner pot of the Instant Pot. Layer sauerkraut over chicken. Add cheese. Top with salad dressing. Sprinkle with parsley.

2. Secure the lid and cook on the Slow Cook setting on low 6 to 8 hours.

Creamy Nutmeg Chicken

Amber Swarey

Makes 6 servings

1 tablespoon canola oil

6 boneless chicken breast halves, skin and visible fat removed

¼ cup chopped onion

¼ cup minced parsley

2 (10¾-ounce) cans 98% fat-free, reduced-sodium cream of mushroom soup

½ cup fat-free sour cream

½ cup fat-free milk

1 tablespoon ground nutmeg

¼ teaspoon sage

¼ teaspoon dried thyme

¼ teaspoon crushed rosemary

1. Press the Sauté button on the Instant Pot and then add the canola oil. Place the chicken in the oil and brown chicken on both sides. Remove the chicken to a plate.

2. Sauté the onion and parsley in the remaining oil in the Instant Pot until the onions are tender. Press Cancel on the Instant Pot, then place the chicken back inside.

3. Mix together the remaining ingredients in a bowl then pour over the chicken.

4. Secure the lid and set the vent to sealing. Set on Manual mode for 10 minutes on high pressure.

5. When cooking time is up, let the pressure release naturally.

BBQ Chicken Tenders

Bryan Woolley

Makes 4–6 servings

1 cup sugar

1 stick (8 tablespoons) butter, melted

½ cup corn syrup

1½ cups water, divided

1 cup diced onion

4 cloves garlic, minced

2 cups prepared barbecue sauce

15 chicken tenders

1 tablespoon Spice Rub

1. Add the sugar, butter, corn syrup, ½ cup water, onion, garlic, and barbecue sauce to the Instant Pot. Stir everything together.

2. Pressure cook on high for 10 minutes, letting the steam release naturally.

3. When the steam has released, transfer the sauce to a bowl and add the chicken tenders to the Instant Pot with 1 cup of water. Secure the lid and pressure cook on high for 5 minutes, letting the pressure release naturally.

4. When the steam has released, remove the lid and transfer the chicken tenders to a large bowl. Sprinkle with 1 tablespoon of the Spice Rub for Chicken Tenders (recipe on page 126) and toss to coat.

5. Drizzle the chicken tenders with the sauce, toss, and serve with your favorite vegetables and enjoy!

Spice Rub for Chicken Tenders

2 tablespoons dried parsley

2 teaspoons dried dill

1 tablespoon onion powder

1 tablespoon garlic powder

1 teaspoon paprika

¼ teaspoon cayenne pepper

2 teaspoons salt

2 teaspoons pepper

1. Combine all the ingredients in a small bowl and mix together. Use as needed.

Lemon Caper Chicken with Egg Noodles

Bryan Woolley

Makes 4 servings

2 pounds egg noodles

2 tablespoons freshly chopped rosemary

¼ cup freshly chopped basil

2 cups white wine

2 cups chicken stock

2 tablespoons freshly squeezed lemon juice

5 tablespoons cold butter, cut into tablespoon pieces

2 chicken breasts, flattened to ¼-inch thick

½ cup capers

Salt to taste

Ground pepper to taste

Red bell pepper, optional

Lemon slice, optional

1. Place egg noodles, rosemary, basil, white wine, chicken stock, and lemon juice into the Instant Pot.

2. Secure lid and pressure cook on high for 2 minutes. Allow steam to release naturally.

3. When steam has released, remove lid and gently stir in butter 1 tablespoon at a time.

4. Place chicken breasts on top of egg noodles and sprinkle with capers and salt and pepper to taste. Secure lid and steam cook for 8 minutes, allowing steam to release naturally.

5. Remove chicken breast and set aside.

6. Divide egg noodles and sauce between four pasta plates.

7. Cut chicken breasts into 4 portions. Serve on top of noodles with a sprinkle of freshly chopped red bell pepper and a lemon slice, if desired.

Thai Chicken and Noodles

Vonnie Oyer

Makes 4 servings

Thai peanut sauce

¾ cup light coconut milk

½ cup peanut butter

2 tablespoons sesame oil

¼ cup fresh lime juice

2 tablespoons soy sauce

1½ teaspoons crushed red pepper flakes

1 tablespoon seasoned rice vinegar

1 tablespoon honey

¼ teaspoon ground ginger

1½ pounds boneless skinless chicken breasts

1½ cups chicken broth

8 ounces dry rice noodles

5 ounces sugar snap peas (about 1½ cups)

1. Mix all the sauce ingredients in a blender. Makes 2 cups (this recipe uses 1 cup).

2. To the inner pot of the Instant Pot, add the chicken, 1 cup Thai peanut sauce, and broth.

3. Secure the lid and make sure vent is at sealing. Cook on Manual at high pressure for 12 minutes.

4. Do a quick release (manual) of the pressure. Remove the chicken from pot, leaving the sauce.

5. To the sauce, add the noodles and ensure all of the dry noodles are submerged in sauce. Top with the peas and replace the cover as quickly as possible.

6. Change the setting to Slow Cook and cook for 10 minutes, or until the noodles are soft but firm.

7. Meanwhile, shred the chicken breasts and set aside.

8. When cook time is up, remove the lid of the Instant Pot and give the noodles a good stir. Stir the chicken back into the inner pot with the noodles.

Thai Chicken Rice Bowls

Vonnie Oyer

Makes 4–6 servings

2 tablespoons olive oil

2 pounds chicken breasts
  (about 4 breasts)

½ cup sweet chili Thai sauce

3 tablespoons soy sauce

½ tablespoon fish sauce

½ tablespoon minced ginger

½ tablespoon minced garlic

1 teaspoon lime juice

1 teaspoon sriracha sauce

1 tablespoon peanut butter

1 cup uncooked long-grain
  white rice

2 cups broth

Cilantro, shredded carrots,
  and peanuts to garnish,
  optional

1. Select the Sauté setting on the Instant Pot and add the olive oil to the inner pot.

2. Sear the chicken for 2–3 minutes on both sides to seal in their juices. Remove to a glass baking dish and turn off the Instant Pot.

3. Mix the sweet chili Thai sauce, soy sauce, fish sauce, ginger, garlic, lime juice, sriracha, and peanut butter together.

4. Pour the sauce over the chicken breasts in glass dish.

5. Place the rice in the inner pot of the Instant Pot and add the chicken and sauce over top.

6. Add the broth and secure the lid. Make sure vent is on sealing.

7. Select the Manual setting on high pressure and set the timer to 10 minutes. Let pressure release naturally.

8. Take out and shred the chicken with two forks. Mix the chicken back in with the rice.

9. Garnish with cilantro, shredded carrots, and peanuts, if desired.

Chicken, Broccoli and Rice

Jessica Stoner

Makes 4 servings

2 tablespoons butter

1½–2 pounds boneless skinless chicken breast, cut into cubes

2 cloves garlic

1 small onion, chopped

1⅓ cups long-grain rice

1⅓ cups chicken broth

1 teaspoon salt

¾ teaspoon pepper

1 teaspoon garlic powder

½ cup milk

1½ tablespoons flour

1–2 cups fresh broccoli, cooked

1½–2 cups shredded mild cheddar cheese

1. Turn Instant Pot to Sauté. Add butter to the inner pot and heat until hot. When hot, add chicken, garlic, and onion.

2. Cook chicken mixture until onion starts to get translucent. Add rice, broth, and seasonings. Stir well.

3. Whisk together milk and flour and set aside.

4. Secure the lid and make sure vent is at sealing. Cook on Manual on high pressure for 5 minutes. When time is up, perform a quick release.

5. Remove lid and immediately add milk and flour mixture and mix until it is well combined.

6. Add broccoli and cheese and stir until well combined. Serve immediately.

Chicken with Spiced Sesame Sauce

Colleen Heatwole

Makes 4–6 servings

2 tablespoons tahini (sesame sauce)

¼ cup water

1 tablespoon soy sauce

¼ cup chopped onion

1 teaspoon red wine vinegar

2 teaspoons minced garlic

1 teaspoon shredded ginger root (using a Microplane works best)

2 pounds chicken breast, chopped into 8 portions

1. Place first seven ingredients in bottom of the inner pot of the Instant Pot.

2. Add coarsely chopped chicken on top.

3. Secure the lid and make sure vent is at sealing. Set for 8 minutes using Manual setting on high pressure. When cook time is up, let the pressure release naturally for 10 minutes, then perform a quick release.

4. Remove ingredients and shred chicken with forks. Combine with other ingredients in pot for a tasty sandwich filling or sauce.

Szechuan-Style Chicken and Broccoli

Jane Meiser

Makes 4 servings

1 tablespoon canola oil

2 whole boneless, skinless chicken breasts, cut into 1-inch cubes

2 cups broccoli florets

1 medium red bell pepper, sliced

½ cup picante sauce

½ cup low-sodium chicken stock

2 tablespoons light soy sauce

½ teaspoon sugar

2 teaspoons quick-cooking tapioca

1 medium onion, chopped

2 cloves garlic, minced

½ teaspoon ground ginger

1. Set the Instant Pot to Sauté and add the oil and chicken. Sauté until lightly browned. Press Cancel.

2. Add in the broccoli and bell pepper. In a small bowl, mix together the remaining ingredients, then pour over the contents of the Instant Pot and stir.

3. Secure the lid and make sure vent is at sealing. Cook in Manual mode on high pressure for 12 minutes.

4. When cooking time is over, let the pressure release naturally for 5 minutes, then release the rest manually.

Sweet-and-Sour Chicken over Rice

Bryan Woolley

Makes 6–8 servings

Olive oil for the pot

4 chicken breasts, cut into 1-inch pieces

1 cup chicken stock

2 large onions, sliced

1 bell pepper, cut into 1-inch pieces

1 bunch green onions, sliced

1 (8-oz.) can pineapple chunks, drained (reserve juice)

¾ cup sugar

½ cup red wine vinegar

2 tablespoons cornstarch (mix with reserved pineapple juice)

Salt to taste

Pepper to taste

1. Select Sauté mode on the Instant Pot. Add just enough olive oil to lightly coat bottom of the pot.

2. Add the chicken pieces to the pot and sauté for 2 minutes, or until they have a little color on them.

3. Pour chicken stock into the Instant Pot and secure the lid. Pressure cook on high for 10 minutes. Use a quick steam release to release the pressure.

4. Once steam is released, remove lid. Add onion slices, bell pepper, green onions, pineapple chunks, sugar, red wine vinegar, and the cornstarch/pineapple juice mixture. Stir to incorporate everything.

5. Pressure cook on low for 5 minutes and use a quick-release method to release the pressure.

6. Season with salt and pepper to taste. Serve sweet-and-sour chicken mixture over rice. Use the Perfect White Rice (page 226) or Best Brown Rice recipe (page 230).

Chicken and Dumplings

Bryan Woolley

Makes 4–6 servings

4 tablespoons butter

Extra-virgin olive oil for the pot

2 chicken breasts, cut into bite-sized pieces

1 large onion, minced

2 cloves garlic, minced

2 cups sliced mushrooms

1 (10-oz.) package frozen peas and carrots

¼ cup flour

2 cups milk

4 cups chicken stock

1 tablespoon dried sage

Salt to taste

Pepper to taste

Dumplings

2 cups all-purpose flour

1 tablespoon baking powder

1 tablespoon sugar

1½ teaspoons salt

⅓ cup lard, shortening, or butter

½ cup milk (or more if needed)

1 egg

1 tablespoon freshly chopped chives

½ teaspoon black pepper

1. Heat Instant Pot on Sauté mode. Add butter and drizzle enough olive oil to lightly coat bottom of pot.

2. Add chopped chicken breasts, onion, garlic, and mushrooms to the Instant Pot. Sauté chicken mixture for 5 minutes. When you start to see color on the chicken pieces, add frozen peas and carrots.

3. Sprinkle flour over top of chicken mixture. Gently stir to incorporate flour into oil.

4. Add milk, chicken stock, sage, and salt and pepper (to taste), stirring everything together to combine. Stir and secure Instant Pot lid. Pressure cook on high for 15 minutes.

5. To make the dumplings, combine all-purpose flour, baking powder, sugar, and 1 teaspoon of the salt into a large mixing bowl and mix together. Next, cut cold lard, shortening, or butter into dry ingredients until it resembles cornmeal. (I like to do this in my food processor with the blade attachment and pulse it a few times until the fat has been cut into dry ingredients.)

6. Then mix in milk, egg, chives, remaining salt, and black pepper and set aside until needed.

7. When pressure cooker is finished, quick release pressure and remove lid.

8. Spoon dumpling mixture on top of soup one spoonful at a time.

9. Place lid back onto pressure cooker and secure in place. Change Instant Pot setting to Steam. Let steam for 10 minutes. Let pressure release naturally.

Mild Chicken Curry with Coconut Milk

Brittney Horst

Makes 4–6 servings

1 large onion, diced

6 cloves garlic, crushed

¼ cup coconut oil (butter or avocado oil would work fine, too)

½ teaspoon black pepper

½ teaspoon turmeric

½ teaspoon paprika

¼ teaspoon cinnamon

¼ teaspoon cloves

¼ teaspoon cumin

¼ teaspoon ginger

½ teaspoon salt

1 tablespoon curry powder (or more if you like more flavor)

½ teaspoon chili powder

1 (24-oz.) can diced or crushed tomatoes

1 (13½-oz.) can coconut milk (I prefer a brand without unwanted ingredients like guar gum or sugar)

4 pounds boneless skinless chicken breasts, cut into chunks

1. Sauté onion and garlic in oil, either with Sauté setting in the inner pot of the Instant Pot, or on stove top and add to pot.

2. Combine spices in a small bowl, then add to the inner pot.

3. Add tomatoes and coconut milk and stir.

4. Add chicken, and stir to coat the pieces with the sauce.

5. Secure the lid and make sure vent is at sealing. Set to Manual mode (or Pressure Cook on newer models) for 14 minutes on high pressure.

6. Let pressure release naturally (or, if you're crunched for time, you can do a quick release).

7. Serve with your favorite sides, and enjoy!

Serving suggestion:

We like it on rice, with a couple of veggies on the side.

Cheesy Stuffed Cabbage

Maria Shevlin

Makes 6–8 servings

1–2 heads savoy cabbage

Water to boil cabbage

1 pound ground turkey

1 egg

1 cup shredded cheddar cheese

2 tablespoons heavy cream

¼ cup shredded Parmesan cheese

¼ cup shredded mozzarella cheese

¼ cup finely diced onion

¼ cup finely diced bell pepper

¼ cup finely diced mushrooms

1 teaspoon salt

½ teaspoon black pepper

1 teaspoon garlic powder

6 basil leaves, fresh and cut chiffonade

1 tablespoon fresh parsley, chopped

1 quart your favorite pasta sauce

1. Remove the core from the cabbages.

2. Boil water and place 1 head at a time into the water for approximately 10 minutes.

3. Allow cabbage to cool slightly. Once cooled, remove the leaves carefully and set aside. You'll need about 15 or 16.

4. Mix together the meat and all remaining ingredients except the pasta sauce.

5. One leaf at a time, put a heaping tablespoon of meat mixture in the center.

6. Tuck the sides in and then roll tightly.

7. Add ½ cup sauce to the bottom of the inner pot of the Instant Pot.

8. Place the rolls, fold side down, into the pot and layer them, putting a touch of sauce between each layer and finally on top. (You may want to cook the rolls half a batch at a time.)

9. Lock lid and make sure vent is at sealing. Set timer for 18 minutes on Manual at high pressure, then manually release the pressure when cook time is over.

Taylor's Favorite Uniquely Stuffed Peppers

Maria Shevlin

Makes 4 servings

4 red bell peppers

1 teaspoon olive oil

½ onion, chopped

3 cloves garlic, minced

½ pound ground turkey

½ pound spicy Italian sausage

1 teaspoon salt

½ teaspoon black pepper

1 teaspoon garlic powder

½ teaspoon dried oregano

½ teaspoon dried basil

1 medium zucchini, grated and water pressed out

½ cup your favorite barbecue sauce

¼ cup quick oats

1 cup water or bone broth

1. Cut the stem part of the top off the bell peppers, remove seeds and membranes, and set aside.

2. Add olive oil, onion, and garlic to a pan. Cook until al dente.

3. Add in ground turkey and sausage, and brown lightly.

4. Add in seasonings, zucchini, and barbecue sauce.

5. Add in oats.

6. Mix well to combine.

7. Stuff the filling inside each pepper—pack it in.

8. Add water or bone broth to the bottom of the inner pot of the Instant Pot.

9. Add the rack to the pot. Arrange the stuffed peppers standing upright in the pot.

10. Lock lid, make sure vent is at sealing, and use the Manual setting to set for 15 minutes on high pressure.

11. When cook time is up, release the pressure manually.

Ground Turkey Cacciatore Spaghetti

Maria Shevlin

Makes 6 servings

1 teaspoon olive oil

1 medium sweet onion, chopped

3 cloves garlic, minced

1 pound ground turkey

1 (32-oz.) jar spaghetti sauce (or 1 quart homemade)

1 teaspoon salt

½ teaspoon black pepper

½ teaspoon oregano

½ teaspoon dried basil

½ teaspoon red pepper flakes

1 cup bell pepper strips, mixed colors if desired

1 cup diced mushrooms

1 (13¼-oz.) box Dreamfield spaghetti

3 cups chicken bone broth

1. Press the Sauté button on the Instant Pot and add the oil, onion, and garlic to the inner pot.

2. Add in the ground turkey and break it up a little while it browns.

3. Once ground turkey is browned, add in the sauce and seasonings.

4. Add in the bell peppers and mushrooms and give it a stir to mix.

5. Add in the spaghetti—break it in half to fit it inside pot.

6. Add in the chicken bone broth.

7. Lock lid, make sure the vent is at sealing, and set on Manual at high pressure for 6 minutes.

8. When cook time is up, manually release the pressure.

Serving suggestion:

Top with some fresh grated Parmesan cheese and basil.

Turkey Meatballs and Gravy

Betty Sue Good

Makes 10 servings

2 eggs, beaten

¾ cup bread crumbs

½ cup finely chopped onion

½ cup finely chopped celery

2 tablespoons chopped fresh parsley

¼ teaspoon pepper

⅛ teaspoon garlic powder

1½ pounds ground turkey

1½ tablespoons canola oil

1 (10¾-oz.) can 99% fat-free, reduced-sodium cream of mushroom soup

1 cup water

1 (⅞-oz.) package turkey gravy mix

½ teaspoon dried thyme

2 bay leaves

1. Combine eggs, bread crumbs, onion, celery, parsley, pepper, garlic powder, and meat. Shape into ¾-inch balls.

2. Set the Instant Pot to Sauté and add in the oil. Lightly brown meatballs in the oil in as many batches as needed. As the meatballs are browned, let them drain on a paper towel–lined plate or dish, then pat dry.

3. When all the meatballs are browned, press Cancel on the Instant Pot and then wipe out the inside of the inner pot. Place the meatballs back inside.

4. Combine soup, water, dry gravy mix, thyme, and bay leaves in a bowl, then pour over the meatballs.

5. Secure the lid and make sure the vent is set to sealing. Press the Manual button and set for 10 minutes on high pressure.

6. When cook time is up, let the pressure release naturally. Discard bay leaves before serving.

Serving suggestion:

Serve over mashed potatoes or buttered noodles.

Turkey Sloppy Joes

Marla Folkerts

Makes 6 servings

1 tablespoon olive oil

1 red onion, chopped

1 bell pepper, chopped

1½ pounds boneless turkey, finely chopped

1 cup ketchup, no salt added

½ teaspoons salt

1 clove garlic, minced

1 teaspoon Dijon-style mustard

⅛ teaspoon pepper

6 multigrain sandwich rolls (1½ oz. each)

1. Set the Instant Pot to Sauté and add the olive oil. Once the olive oil is hot, add in the onion, bell pepper, and turkey. Sauté until the turkey is brown. Press Cancel.

2. Combine ketchup, salt, garlic, mustard, and pepper, then pour over the turkey mixture. Mix well.

3. Secure the lid and make sure the vent is set to sealing. Put the Instant Pot on Manual mode for 15 minutes on high pressure.

4. When cook time is up, let the pressure release naturally for 5 minutes, then perform a quick release. Serve on sandwich rolls.

Daddy's Pasta Fasool

Maria Shevlin

Makes 8 servings

1 cup tomato sauce

1 cup diced onion

½ cup diced carrots

½ cup diced celery

1 tablespoon chopped fresh celery leaves

1 (14½-oz.) can petite diced tomatoes

1 cup precooked ground turkey

3–4 cloves garlic, minced

1 bay leaf

½ teaspoon onion powder

½ teaspoon garlic powder

¼ teaspoon basil

¼ teaspoon oregano

½ teaspoon parsley flakes

½ teaspoon salt

¼ teaspoon black pepper

1 (15½-oz.) can cannelini beans, drained and rinsed (I use Goya brand)

1 cup Dreamfield elbows or similar small pasta of your choice

4 cups chicken bone broth

1. In the inner pot of the Instant Pot, add the sauce, vegetables, tomatoes, meat, and seasonings, and stir.

2. Set to Sauté for 5 minutes, stirring occasionally.

3. After 5 minutes add the beans, pasta, and bone broth, in that order.

4. Lock lid, set vent to sealing, then set on Manual at high pressure for 6 minutes.

5. Release the pressure manually when cooking time is over.

Insta Pasta à la Maria

Maria Shevlin

Makes 6–8 servings

1 (32-oz.) jar your favorite spaghetti sauce (or 1 quart homemade)

2 cups fresh chopped spinach

1 cup chopped mushrooms

½ precooked whole rotisserie chicken, shredded

1 teaspoon salt

½ teaspoon black pepper

½ teaspoon dried basil

¼ teaspoon red pepper flakes

1 teaspoon parsley flakes

1 (13¼-oz.) box pasta, any shape or brand (I used Dreamfield)

3 cups water

1. Place the sauce in the bottom of the inner pot of the Instant Pot.

2. Add in the spinach, then the mushrooms.

3. Add the chicken on top of the veggies and sauce.

4. Add the seasonings and give it a stir to mix.

5. Add the box of pasta.

6. Add water.

7. Secure the lid and move vent to sealing. Set to Manual on high pressure for 6 minutes.

8. When cook time is up, release the pressure manually.

9. Remove the lid and stir to mix together.

Zulu Bread in Chicken Harissa Broth

David Murphy

Makes 6 servings

Dough

1 teaspoon instant dry yeast

4 teaspoons granulated sugar

1 cup warm water

½ teaspoon salt

1 cup all-purpose flour

1 cup cornmeal

Broth

2 tablespoons olive oil

12 ounces chicken sausage, sliced

1 teaspoon sea salt

1 tablespoon harissa paste

4 cups chicken stock

Sea salt to taste

Cracked pepper to taste

1. In a bowl, combine yeast, sugar, and water. Wait 5 to 6 minutes, or until yeast starts to have bubbles. Once bubbles have formed, add in salt, flour, and cornmeal. Mix well until you have a soft ball.

2. Knead dough in bowl until you have a pliable dough; add more water if necessary. Knead for about 10 minutes, or until soft and elastic. Place in a lightly oiled bowl and leave in a warm place to rise for about an hour.

3. Punch the dough and knead for 2 to 3 more minutes. Roll into a round ball of dough. Allow the dough to rise for 5 minutes.

4. While waiting for dough to rise, make harissa broth. Turn pot on to Sauté Normal mode. Add olive oil and wait until heated. Once heated, add chicken sausage. Cook until sausage has a slight sear on it.

5. Add in remaining ingredients. Bring to a slight boil. Once boiling has begun, add your Zulu dough to the center. Cook on Manual at high pressure for 20 minutes and let pressure naturally release for 10 minutes. Quick release any remaining pressure.

6. Remove lid and allow mixture to cool for a minute or two. With a spatula, remove the Zulu bread from the broth and place on cutting board. Serve slices of the bread with the soup.

Zesty Pineapple Chicken

David Murphy

Makes 5 servings

3 pounds boneless skinless chicken breast

1 (12-oz.) jar Trader Joe's Pineapple Salsa

1 (40-oz.) Dole Tropical Gold Pineapple chunks, including the juice from the cans

¼ teaspoon Slap Ya Mama or other Cajun seasoning

1 teaspoons sea salt

1. Place all ingredients into the inner pot of your Instant Pot. Lock the lid and close the vent. Place on Manual at high pressure for 12 minutes, and allow pressure to naturally release

2. Once depressurized, open the vent to ensure that all pressure has been released. Pull out the chicken breasts onto a plate or cutting board, and shred with forks.

3. Once the chicken is shredded, add it back into your Instant Pot. Let it set for a couple of minutes to marinate in the pineapple juice base before serving.

Beef, Pork & Lamb

Pot Roast

Carol Eveleth

Makes 4 servings

2 pounds beef roast, boneless

¼ teaspoon salt

¼ teaspoon pepper

1 tablespoon olive oil

2 stalks celery, chopped

4 tablespoons butter

2 cups tomato juice

2 cloves garlic, finely chopped, or 1 teaspoon garlic powder

1 teaspoon thyme

1 bay leaf

4 carrots, chopped

1 medium onion, chopped

4 medium potatoes, chopped

1. Pat beef dry with paper towels; season on all sides with ¼ teaspoon each salt and pepper.

2. Select Sauté function on the Instant Pot and adjust heat to "more." Put the oil in the inner pot, then cook the beef in oil for 6 minutes, until browned, turning once. Set on plate.

3. Add celery and butter to the inner pot; cook 2 minutes. Stir in tomato juice, garlic, thyme, and bay leaf. Hit Cancel to turn off Sauté function.

4. Place beef on top of the contents of the inner pot and press into sauce. Cover and lock lid and make sure vent is at sealing. Select Manual and cook at high pressure for 1 hour 15 minutes.

5. Once cooking is complete, release pressure by using natural release function. Transfer beef to cutting board. Discard bay leaf.

6. Skim off any excess fat from surface. Choose Sauté function and adjust heat to "more." Cook 18 minutes, or until reduced by about half (2½ cups). Hit Cancel to turn off Sauté function.

(Continued on next page)

7. Add carrots, onion, and potatoes. Cover and lock lid and make sure vent is at sealing. Select Manual and cook at high pressure for 10 minutes.

8. Once cooking is complete, release pressure by using a quick release. Using Sauté function, keep at a simmer.

9. Season with more salt and pepper to taste.

Serving suggestion:

Serve with a side of steamed broccoli to add some bright color to the dish!

Pot Roast with Tomato Sauce

Carol Eveleth

Makes 4–6 servings

2 pounds beef roast, boneless

¼ teaspoon salt

¼ teaspoon pepper

1 tablespoon olive oil

2 stalks celery, chopped

4 tablespoons margarine

2 cups low-sodium tomato juice

2 cloves garlic, finely chopped, or 1 teaspoon garlic powder

1 teaspoon thyme

1 bay leaf

4 carrots, chopped

1 medium onion, chopped

4 medium potatoes, chopped

1. Pat beef dry with paper towels; season on all sides with salt and pepper.

2. Select Sauté function on the Instant Pot and adjust heat to more. Put the oil in the inner pot, then cook the beef in oil for 6 minutes, until browned, turning once. Set on plate.

3. Add celery and margarine to the inner pot; cook 2 minutes. Stir in tomato juice, garlic, thyme, and bay leaf. Hit Cancel to turn off Sauté function.

4. Place beef on top of the contents of the inner pot and press into sauce. Cover and lock lid and make sure vent is at sealing. Select Manual and cook at high pressure for 1 hour 15 minutes.

5. Once cooking is complete, release pressure by using natural release function. Transfer beef to cutting board. Discard bay leaf.

6. Skim off any excess fat from surface. Choose Sauté function and adjust heat to more. Cook 18 minutes, or until reduced by about half (2½ cups). Hit Cancel to turn off Sauté function.

(Continued on next page)

7. Add carrots, onion, and potatoes. Cover and lock lid and make sure vent is at sealing. Select Manual and cook at high pressure for 10 minutes.

8. Once cooking is complete, release pressure by using a quick release. Using Sauté function, keep at a simmer.

9. Season with more salt and pepper to taste.

Serving suggestion:

Brighten this dish up with some colorful, freshly steamed broccoli when serving.

Easy Pot Roast and Vegetables

Tina Houk, Arlene Wines

Makes 6 servings

3–4 pounds chuck roast, trimmed of fat and cut into serving-sized chunks

4 medium potatoes, cubed, unpeeled

4 medium carrots, sliced (or 1 pound baby carrots)

2 celery ribs, sliced thin

1 envelope dry onion soup mix

3 cups water

1. Place the pot roast chunks into the Instant Pot along with the potatoes, carrots, and celery.

2. Mix together the onion soup mix and water and pour over the contents of the Instant Pot.

3. Secure the lid and make sure the vent is set to sealing. Set the Instant Pot to Manual mode for 35 minutes on high pressure. Let pressure release naturally when cook time is up.

Variation:

Before putting roast in cooker, sprinkle it with the dry soup mix, patting it on so it adheres.

Pork Butt Roast

Marla Folkerts

Makes 6–8 servings

3–4-pounds pork butt roast

2–3 tablespoons your favorite rub

2 cups water

1. Place pork in the inner pot of the Instant Pot.

2. Sprinkle the rub all over the roast and add the water, being careful not to wash off the rub.

3. Secure the lid and set the vent to sealing. Cook for 9 minutes on the Manual setting on high pressure.

4. Let the pressure release naturally.

Pulled Pork

Colleen Heatwole

Makes 8 servings

2 tablespoons vegetable oil

1 (4-lb.) boneless pork shoulder, cut into two pieces

2 cups barbecue sauce, divided

½ cup water

1. Add oil to the inner pot of the Instant Pot and select Sauté.

2. When oil is hot, brown pork on both sides, about 3 minutes per side. Brown each half of roast separately. Remove to platter when browned.

3. Add 1 cup barbecue sauce and water to the inner pot. Stir to combine.

4. Add browned pork and any accumulated juices to the inner pot. Secure the lid and set vent to sealing.

5. Using Meat/Stew mode, set timer to 60 minutes, on high pressure.

6. When cook time is up, allow the pressure to release naturally.

7. Carefully remove meat and shred with two forks, discarding excess fat as you shred.

8. Strain cooking liquid, reserving ½ cup. If possible, use fat separator to separate fat from juices.

9. Place shredded pork in the inner pot with remaining 1 cup barbecue sauce and reserved ½ cup cooking liquid. Using Sauté function, stir to combine and bring to a simmer, stirring frequently.

Serving suggestion:

We serve on toasted buns. Our barbecue sauce of choice is Sweet Baby Ray's.

BBQ Pork Sandwiches

Carol Eveleth

Makes 4 servings

2 teaspoons salt

1 teaspoon onion powder

1 teaspoon garlic powder

1 (2-lb.) pork shoulder roast, cut into 3-inch pieces

1 tablespoon olive oil

2 cups barbecue sauce

1. In a small bowl, combine the salt, onion powder, and garlic powder. Season the pork with the rub.

2. Turn the Instant Pot on to Sauté. Heat the olive oil in the inner pot.

3. Add the pork to the oil and turn to coat. Lock the lid and set vent to sealing.

4. Press Manual and cook on high pressure for 45 minutes.

5. When cooking is complete, release the pressure manually, then open the lid.

6. Using 2 forks, shred the pork, pour barbecue sauce over top, then press Sauté. Simmer 3 to 5 minutes. Press Cancel. Toss pork to mix.

Serving suggestion:

Pile the shredded BBQ pork on the bottom half of a bun. Add any additional toppings if you wish, then finish with the top half of the bun.

Philippine Ulam

Carol Eveleth

Makes 4–6 servings

2 pounds cubed pork chunks

¼ teaspoon black pepper

1–2 tablespoons oil

4 cups cubed potatoes

3 bell peppers, diced

¼ cup lemon juice

½ cup soy sauce

4 cups water

1. Sprinkle pork chunks with pepper.

2. Press Sauté. When the word "hot" appears, swirl in oil in the inner pot.

3. Place the cubed pork chunks in the inner pot and cook 5 minutes, or until golden brown on all sides.

4. Add cubed potatoes, peppers, lemon juice, soy sauce, and water.

5. Close and lock the lid of the Instant Pot. Turn the steam release handle to sealing position. Cook on Manual at high pressure for 20 minutes. Allow a 10-minute natural pressure release. Turn steam release handle to venting to release remaining pressure.

Serving suggestion:

Serve over cooked rice.

Hawaiian-Style Kalua Pork and Rice

Bryan Woolley

Makes 6–8 servings

1 (4-lb.) pork shoulder roast

1 tablespoon sea salt

1 teaspoon liquid smoke

6 cups vegetable stock

4 cups rice

1 cup water

1. Cut pork shoulder roast in half and sprinkle with sea salt. Set aside.

2. Add liquid smoke (be careful because a little goes a long way) and vegetable stock to Instant Pot.

3. Place steam rack into pot and place pork shoulder roast on top of steam rack.

4. Secure lid and pressure cook on high for 90 minutes. Let pressure release naturally.

5. Using two forks, check pork shoulder roast for tenderness. If you can't easily shred it, secure Instant Pot lid again and pressure cook on high for an additional 15 minutes. Repeat as needed.

6. When roast is easy to shred, transfer entire roast and liquid to large bowl and set aside.

7. Add 4 cups rice to Instant Pot bowl. Add 4 cups of the liquid from pork roast and water to rice.

8. Secure lid. Use Rice mode on the Instant Pot to cook rice.

(Continued on next page)

9. If you don't have a Rice mode, pressure cook rice for 8 minutes on low pressure. Let the steam release naturally. Remove lid when steam has released.

10. While rice is cooking, shred pork.

11. I like to serve the shredded pork and rice with green beans, freshly sliced pineapple, and Hawaiian rolls on the side.

Shredded Pork Tostadas with Mashed Potatoes

Bryan Woolley

Makes 6 servings

1 (2-lb.) pork shoulder roast

2 cups vegetable stock

Salt to taste

Pepper to taste

3 large russet potatoes, peeled and cut into pieces

1 cup sharp shredded cheese

12 tostada shells

1 red bell pepper, diced

1 bunch green onions, chopped

2 cups shredded lettuce

1 cup diced tomatoes

Hot sauce

1. To make shredded pork, cut pork roast into 4 equal parts and place in Instant Pot. Pour vegetable stock over it and sprinkle with salt and pepper. Secure Instant Pot lid. Pressure cook on high for 90 minutes.

2. Let pressure release naturally. Remove lid and shred pork with a couple of forks. If needed, you can adjust cooking times longer to make sure pork shreds easily.

3. Remove pork and place potatoes into the drippings of the pork roast.

4. Place lid back on the Instant Pot and pressure cook on high for 5 minutes. Let the steam release naturally when finished.

5. Remove potatoes using a slotted spoon or strainer.

6. Place potatoes into a large bowl along with shredded cheese. Mash together. Adjust salt and pepper to taste.

7. To assemble tostadas, place a dollop of mashed potatoes followed by some shredded pork, sprinkling of diced red bell pepper, green onions, shredded lettuce, and diced tomatoes on top of a prepared tostada shell. Serve with your favorite hot sauce.

Pork Tamales

Bryan Woolley

Makes 6–8 servings

Olive oil for pot

1 (3-lb.) bone-in pork roast

1 teaspoon salt

1 teaspoon black pepper

5 cups vegetable stock

1 package dried corn husks

½ cup lard

4 cups Maseca corn flour

1 cup frozen corn

⅓ cup chopped green chilies

1 cup water

1. Heat Instant Pot on Sauté mode. Add enough oil to lightly coat bottom of pot.

2. Place pork roast into the pot. Sprinkle with salt and pepper. Brown all sides of roast.

3. Pour vegetable stock over roast. Secure Instant Pot lid.

4. Pressure cook on high for 90 minutes. Let steam release naturally. Reserve the pork drippings to make the masa in step 8.

5. While roast is cooking, place dried corn husks in a large bowl of water. Weigh them down so they rehydrate and become pliable (about 30 minutes).

6. When roast is cooked, shred with a couple of forks.

7. To make masa, cream lard until light and fluffy using mixer with paddle attachment. Add Maseca corn flour, frozen corn, and green chilies. Mix everything together.

8. Add 1 to 2 cups of the pork roast drippings, mixing until a soft dough is formed.

(Continued on next page)

9. Place a generous portion of prepared masa onto the upper center of wide end of corn husk. Place a large piece of shredded pork over masa. Fold sides over and bring bottom portion of husk up over the masa. Repeat to make about a dozen tamales, depending on their size.

10. Place steam rack into Instant Pot and place the tamales open end up on top of the steam rack. You should have enough tamales to support each other upright in pot. Pour 1 cup water into bottom of pot. Secure lid.

11. Pressure cook on low for 30 minutes. Let steam release naturally. Remove lid.

12. Gently remove tamales. Serve with your favorite salsa on the side.

Collard Greens with Ham Hocks

David Murphy

Makes 6 servings

2 bunches collard greens, triple washed and veins removed, rough chopped

1 cup chicken broth

1 cup water

2 ham hocks

1 tablespoon garlic, minced

2 tablespoons Cholula or your favorite hot sauce

2 tablespoons apple cider vinegar

Sea salt to taste

Cracked pepper to taste

1. Add all ingredients into your pot, layering ham hocks on top of greens. Set on Manual at high pressure for 16 minutes, then quick release all pressure.

2. Remove ham hocks from pot and pull meat off the bone and add back to the pot before serving. Make the Jalapeño Bacon Corn Bread (page 16) to enjoy with it!

Tender Tasty Ribs

Carol Eveleth

Makes 2–3 servings

2 teaspoons salt

2 teaspoons black pepper

1 teaspoon garlic powder

1 teaspoon onion powder

1 slab baby back ribs

1 cup water

1 cup barbecue sauce,
divided

1. Mix salt, pepper, garlic powder, and onion powder together. Rub seasoning mixture on both sides of slab of ribs. Cut slab in half if it's too big for your Instant Pot.

2. Pour water into inner pot of the Instant Pot. Place ribs into pot, drizzle with ¼ cup of sauce, and secure lid. Make sure the vent is set to sealing.

3. Set it to Manual for 25 minutes on high pressure. It will take a few minutes to heat up and seal the vent. When cook time is up, let it sit 5 minutes, then release steam by turning valve to venting. Turn oven on to broil (or heat your grill) while you're waiting for the 5-minute resting time.

4. Remove ribs from Instant Pot and place on a baking sheet. Slather both sides with remaining ¾ cup sauce.

5. Place under broiler (or on grill) for 5 to 10 minutes, watching carefully so it doesn't burn. Remove and brush with a bit more sauce. Pull apart and dig in!

Pork Baby Back Ribs

Marla Folkerts

Makes 6–8 servings

3 racks of ribs

1 cup brown sugar

1 cup white sugar

1 teaspoon garlic powder

1 teaspoon garlic salt

1 cup water

½ cup apple cider vinegar

1 teaspoon liquid smoke

½ cup barbecue sauce

1. Take the membrane/skin off the back of the ribs.

2. Mix together the remaining ingredients (except the barbecue sauce) and slather it on the ribs.

3. Place the ribs around the inside of the inner pot instead of stacking them. Secure the lid in place and make sure vent is at sealing.

4. Use the Meat setting and set for 30 minutes on high pressure.

5. When cooking time is up, let the pressure release naturally for 10 minutes, then do a quick release of the remaining pressure.

6. Place the ribs on a baking sheet and cover them with the barbecue sauce. Broil for 7 to 10 minutes (watching so they don't burn).

Country Pork Ribs

Bryan Woolley

Makes 6–8 serivngs

3–4 pounds country-style pork ribs

2 cups prepared barbecue sauce

2 cups chicken stock

1 cup apricot jam

1 tablespoon smoked paprika

1 tablespoon garlic powder

1 tablespoon onion powder

1 tablespoon chili powder

1 tablespoon herbes de Provence

Salt to taste

Freshly cracked pepper to taste

Pork Gravy

⅓ cup flour

½ cup water

Pork drippings

1. Place country-style pork ribs into the Instant Pot. (Country-style pork ribs are boneless pork ribs.)

2. Add the barbecue sauce, chicken stock, apricot jam, smoked paprika, garlic powder, onion powder, chili powder, and herbes de Provence.

3. Gently stir everything together. Secure lid onto the Instant Pot. Pressure cook on high for 45 minutes. Allow pressure to release naturally.

4. Use pork drippings to make a pork gravy: make a flour slurry by combining flour and water together. Pour into the pork drippings.

5. Bring drippings to a boil until they thicken. Strain gravy if needed. Adjust seasonings to taste and enjoy. Serve with Mashed Potatoes (page 207).

Teriyaki Ribs

Janie Steele

Makes 2–3 servings

½ tablespoon chopped ginger

1 cup beef broth

½ cup soy sauce

1 tablespoon minced garlic

4 tablespoons brown sugar

2 tablespoons sriracha sauce (or more to taste)

⅓ cup hoisin sauce

1–2 pounds rack of ribs

1. Mix all ingredients together in a bowl, except the ribs.

2. Cut ribs into smaller 2- to 3-rib sections and place in bottom of the inner pot of the Instant Pot.

3. Pour the sauce on top.

4. Secure the lid and make sure vent is at sealing. Set to Manual and cook on high pressure for 25 minutes.

5. Let the pressure release naturally.

6. Serve as is, or if you want crispier coating, set oven to 375°F and bake for about 5 minutes.

7. Reserve sauce from pot as desired for dipping.

Kimchi Pork Dim Sum

Bryan Woolley

Makes 6–8 servings

1 pound ground pork

1 cup chopped kimchi

1 teaspoon ginger

1 teaspoon granulated garlic

2 tablespoons soy sauce

2 tablespoons brown sugar

¼ cup freshly chopped chives

½ cup finely chopped onion

1 egg

1 tablespoon water + 1 cup

Egg roll wrappers

Dipping sauce

¼ cup soy sauce

2 teaspoons toasted sesame seed oil

¼ cup chopped chives

1 tablespoon brown sugar

½ teaspoon red pepper flakes

1. In a large bowl, add pork, kimchi, ginger, garlic, soy sauce, brown sugar, chives, and onion. Mix everything together to combine.

2. Whisk egg with 1 tablespoon of water in a small bowl and set aside. Place an egg roll wrapper on a flat working surface and lightly brush the edges with egg wash.

3. Spoon 2 to 3 tablespoons of kimchi-pork filling onto center of egg wrapper. Fold each egg roll wrapper in half, pressing down to seal edges.

4. Gently press bottom of dim sum onto flat surface to create a flat bottom.

5. When ready, place steam rack in bottom of Instant Pot. Add 1 cup water. Spray bamboo steamer basket with vegetable spray and place it down onto the steam rack. (I use a round, stackable bamboo steamer that fits into the Instant Pot.)

6. Secure lid of Instant Pot and steam for 8 minutes, letting steam release naturally.

7. Transfer dim sum to a serving dish.

8. To make dipping sauce, add ingredients to a small bowl, whisking everything together. Serve dipping sauce with kimchi pork dim sum.

Beef Pot Stickers

David Murphy

Makes 48

4 green onions, thinly sliced

2 tablespoons reduced-sodium soy sauce

2 cloves garlic, minced

1 tablespoon rice vinegar

1 tablespoon minced fresh ginger root

¼ teaspoon coarsely ground pepper

1 pound ground beef

48 pot sticker or gyoza wrappers

2 cups water

1. In a large bowl, combine all ingredients except the beef, wrappers, and 2 cups water. Add beef; mix lightly and thoroughly. Place a teaspoon of filling in the center of each wrapper. Moisten wrapper edges with some water. Fold wrapper over filling; seal edges to form a pleated pouch. Stand pot stickers on your work surface to flatten bottoms. Keep dumplings covered with a moist cloth until ready to cook.

2. Place 2 cups of water and trivet into your pot, press Steam and allow water to boil. Place dumplings in a steamer basket. Place basket on trivet. Place your Instant Pot glass lid on top and cook for approximately 5 to 6 minutes or until cooked through.

Beef Broccoli

Anita Troyer

Makes 6 servings

1 tablespoon oil

1½ pounds boneless beef, trimmed and sliced thinly (round steak or chuck roast)

¼ teaspoon black pepper

½ cup diced onion

3 cloves garlic, minced

¾ cup beef broth

½ cup soy sauce

¼ cup brown sugar

2 tablespoons sesame oil

¼ teaspoon red pepper flakes

1 pound broccoli, chopped

3 tablespoons water

3 tablespoons cornstarch

Serving suggestion:

Serve over rice.

1. Put oil into the inner pot of the Instant Pot and select Sauté. When oil begins to sizzle, brown the beef in several small batches, taking care to brown well. After browning, remove and put into another bowl. Season with black pepper.

2. Sauté onion in pot for 2 minutes. Add garlic and sauté another minute. Add beef broth, soy sauce, brown sugar, sesame oil, and red pepper flakes. Stir to mix well.

3. Add beef to mixture in inner pot. Secure lid and make sure vent is at sealing. Set on Manual at high pressure and set timer for 12 minutes.

4. After beep, turn cooker off and use quick pressure release. Remove lid.

5. In microwave bowl, steam the broccoli for 3 minutes or until desired doneness.

6. In a small bowl, stir together water and cornstarch. Add to the beef mixture in the Instant Pot and stir. Put on Sauté setting and stir some more. After mixture becomes thick, add broccoli and turn pot off.

Beef Sauerbraten

Bryan Woolley

Makes 6–8 servings

1 cup red wine vinegar

1 cup water

1 large onion, chopped

5 whole cloves

1 tablespoon dry dill

¼ cup sugar

1 tablespoon ground pepper

2 teaspoons salt

3–4 pounds beef roast

1. Add red wine vinegar, water, onion, cloves, dill, sugar, pepper, and salt to the Instant Pot.

2. Set Instant Pot on Sauté and bring mixture to a boil. Stir to dissolve sugar and salt.

3. Place the steam rack into the Instant Pot and the beef roast on top. Secure lid and pressure cook on high for 2 hours.

4. Let pressure release naturally. Remove lid when safe. Check roast for tenderness. Serve with red cabbage, Country-Style Potatoes (page 205), and freshly baked rolls.

Beef Burgundy

Jacqueline Stefl

Makes 6 servings

2 tablespoons olive oil

2 pounds stewing meat, cubed, trimmed of fat

2½ tablespoons flour

5 medium onions, thinly sliced

½ pound fresh mushrooms, sliced

1 teaspoon salt

¼ teaspoon dried marjoram

¼ teaspoon dried thyme

⅛ teaspoon pepper

¾ cup beef broth

1½ cups burgundy

1. Press Sauté on the Instant Pot and add in the olive oil.

2. Dredge meat in flour, then brown in batches in the Instant Pot. Set aside the meat. Sauté the onions and mushrooms in the remaining oil and drippings for about 3–4 minutes, then add the meat back in. Press Cancel.

3. Add the salt, marjoram, thyme, pepper, broth, and wine to the Instant Pot.

4. Secure the lid and make sure the vent is set to sealing. Press the Manual button and set to 30 minutes on high pressure.

5. When cook time is up, let the pressure release naturally for 15 minutes, then perform a quick release.

6. Serve over cooked noodles.

Beef Roast with Mushroom Barley

Sue Hamilton

Makes 6 servings

1 tablespoon olive oil

2 pounds beef chuck roast, visible fat removed

1 cup pearl barley (not quick-cook)

½ cup onion, diced

1 (6½-oz.) can mushrooms, undrained

1 teaspoon minced garlic

1 teaspoon Italian seasoning

¼ teaspoon black pepper

1¾ cups beef broth

1. Press the Sauté button on the Instant Pot and pour the oil in to warm up. Brown the roast for about 5 minutes on each side. Press Cancel.

2. Add the rest of the ingredients to the Instant Pot, then secure the lid, making sure the vent is set to sealing.

3. Press the Manual button and set the time for 1 hour and 15 minutes on high pressure.

4. When cook time is up, let the pressure release naturally for 15 minutes, then perform a quick release.

Serving suggestion:

Serve this with mashed potatoes. They'll benefit from the delicious broth in this dish.

Machaca Beef

Jeanne Allen

Makes 12 servings

1½ pounds beef roast

1 large onion, sliced

1 (4-oz.) can chopped green chilies

2 beef bouillon cubes

1½ teaspoons dry mustard

½ teaspoon garlic powder

1 teaspoon seasoning salt

½ teaspoon pepper

1 cup water

1 cup salsa

1. Combine all ingredients except salsa in the Instant Pot inner pot.

2. Secure the lid and make sure the vent is set to sealing. Press the Slow Cook button and set on low for 12 hours, or until beef is tender. Drain and reserve liquid.

3. Shred beef using two forks to pull it apart.

4. Combine beef, salsa, and enough of the reserved liquid to make desired consistency.

5. Use this filling for burritos, chalupas, quesadillas, or tacos.

Bavarian Beef

Naomi E. Fast

Makes 8 servings

1 tablespoon canola oil

3 pounds boneless beef chuck roast, trimmed of fat

3 cups sliced carrots

3 cups sliced onions

2 large kosher dill pickles, chopped

1 cup sliced celery

½ cup dry red wine or beef broth

⅓ cup German-style mustard

2 teaspoons coarsely ground black pepper

2 bay leaves

¼ teaspoon ground cloves

1 cup water

⅓ cup flour

1. Press Sauté on the Instant Pot and add in the oil. Brown roast on both sides for about 5 minutes. Press Cancel.

2. Add all of the remaining ingredients, except for the flour, to the Instant Pot.

3. Secure the lid and make sure the vent is set to sealing. Press Manual and set the time to 1 hour and 15 minutes on high pressure. Let the pressure release naturally.

4. Remove meat and vegetables to large platter. Cover to keep warm.

5. Remove 1 cup of the liquid from the Instant Pot and mix with the flour. Press Sauté on the Instant Pot and add the flour/broth mixture back in, whisking. Cook until the broth is smooth and thickened.

6. Serve over noodles or spaetzle.

Garlic Beef Stroganoff

Sharon Miller

Makes 6 servings

2 tablespoons canola oil

1½ pounds boneless round steak, cut into thin strips, trimmed of fat

2 teaspoons sodium-free beef bouillon powder

1 cup mushroom juice, with water added to make a full cup

2 (4½-ounce) jars sliced mushrooms, drained with juice reserved

1 (10¾-oz.) can 98% fat-free, lower-sodium cream of mushroom soup

1 large onion, chopped

3 cloves garlic, minced

1 tablespoon Worcestershire sauce

6 ounces fat-free cream cheese, cubed and softened

1. Press the Sauté button and put the oil into the Instant Pot inner pot.

2. Once the oil is heated, sauté the beef until it is lightly browned, about 2 minutes on each side. Set the beef aside for a moment. Press Cancel and wipe out the Instant Pot with some paper towel.

3. Press Sauté again and dissolve the bouillon in the mushroom juice and water in inner pot of the Instant Pot. Once dissolved, press Cancel.

4. Add the mushrooms, soup, onion, garlic, and Worcestershire sauce and stir. Add the beef back to the pot.

5. Secure the lid and make sure the vent is set to sealing. Press Manual and set for 15 minutes on high pressure.

6. When cook time is up, let the pressure release naturally for 15 minutes, then perform a quick release.

7. Press Cancel and remove the lid. Press Sauté. Stir in cream cheese until smooth.

8. Serve over noodles.

Steak Stroganoff

Marie Morucci

Makes 6 servings

1 tablespoon olive oil

2 tablespoons flour

½ teaspoon garlic powder

½ teaspoon pepper

¼ teaspoon paprika

1¾ pounds boneless beef round steak, trimmed of fat, cut into 1½ × ½-inch strips

1 (10¾-oz.) can reduced-sodium, 98% fat-free cream of mushroom soup

½ cup water

1 envelope sodium-free dried onion soup mix

1 (9-oz.) jar sliced mushrooms, drained

½ cup fat-free sour cream

1 tablespoon minced fresh parsley

1. Place the oil in the Instant Pot and press Sauté.

2. Combine flour, garlic powder, pepper, and paprika in a small bowl. Stir the steak pieces through the flour mixture until they are evenly coated.

3. Lightly brown the steak pieces in the oil in the Instant Pot, about 2 minutes each side. Press Cancel when done.

4. Stir the mushroom soup, water, and onion soup mix then pour over the steak.

5. Secure the lid and set the vent to sealing. Press the Manual button and set for 15 minutes on high pressure.

6. When cook time is up, let the pressure release naturally for 15 minutes, then release the rest manually.

7. Remove the lid and press Cancel then Sauté. Stir in mushrooms, sour cream, and parsley. Let the sauce come to a boil and cook for about 10 to 15 minutes.

Zesty Swiss Steak

Marilyn Mowry

Makes 6 servings

3–4 tablespoons flour

½ teaspoon salt

¼ teaspoon pepper

1½ teaspoons dry mustard

1½–2 pounds round steak, trimmed of fat

1 tablespoon canola oil

1 cup sliced onions

1 pound carrots, sliced

1 (14½-oz.) can whole tomatoes

⅓ cup water

1 tablespoon brown sugar

1½ tablespoons Worcestershire sauce

1. Combine flour, salt, pepper, and dry mustard.

2. Cut steak into serving pieces. Dredge in flour mixture.

3. Set the Instant Pot to Sauté and add in the oil. Brown the steak pieces on both sides in the oil. Press Cancel.

4. Add onions and carrots into the Instant Pot.

5. Combine the tomatoes, water, brown sugar, and Worcestershire sauce. Pour into the Instant Pot.

6. Secure the lid and make sure the vent is set to sealing. Press Manual and set the time for 35 minutes on high pressure.

7. When cook time is up, let the pressure release naturally for 15 minutes, then perform a quick release.

Three-Pepper Steak

Renee Hankins

Makes 10 servings

3 pounds beef flank steak, cut in ¼- to ½-inch-thick slices across the grain

3 bell peppers, any combination of colors, cut into ¼-inch-thick slices

2 cloves garlic, sliced

1 large onion, sliced

1 teaspoon ground cumin

½ teaspoon dried oregano

1 bay leaf

¼ cup water

Salt to taste

1 (14½-oz.) can diced tomatoes in juice

Jalapeño chilies, sliced, optional

1. Place all ingredients into the Instant Pot and stir.

2. Sprinkle with jalapeño pepper slices if you wish.

3. Secure the lid and make sure vent is set to sealing. Press Manual and set the time for 15 minutes on high pressure.

4. When cook time is up, let the pressure release naturally for 15 minutes, then perform a quick release of the remaining pressure.

Serving suggestion:

We love this served over noodles, rice, or torn tortillas.

"Smothered" Steak

Susan Yoder Graber

Makes 6 servings

1 tablespoon olive oil

⅓ cup flour

¼ teaspoon pepper

1½ pounds chuck, or round, steak, cut into strips, trimmed of fat

1 large onion, sliced

1 green pepper, sliced

1 (14½-oz.) can stewed tomatoes

1 (4-oz.) can mushrooms, drained

2 tablespoons soy sauce

1 (10-oz.) package frozen French-style green beans

1. Press Sauté and add the oil to the Instant Pot.

2. Mix together the flour and pepper in a small bowl. Place the steak pieces into the mixture in the bowl and coat each of them well.

3. Lightly brown the steak pieces in the Instant Pot, about 2 minutes on each side. Press Cancel when done.

4. Add the remaining ingredients to the Instant Pot and mix together gently.

5. Secure the lid and make sure vent is set to sealing. Press Manual and set for 15 minutes on high pressure.

6. When cook time is up, let the pressure release naturally for 15 minutes, then perform a quick release.

Variations:

1. Use 1 (8-oz.) can tomato sauce instead of stewed tomatoes.

2. Substitute 1 tablespoon Worcestershire sauce in place of soy sauce.

Serving suggestion:

Serve over rice.

Quick Steak Tacos

Hope Comerford

Makes 6 servings

1 tablespoon olive oil

8 ounces sirloin steak

2 tablespoons steak seasoning

1 teaspoon Worcestershire sauce

½ red onion, sliced

6 corn tortillas

¼ cup tomatoes

¾ cup reduced-fat Mexican cheese

2 tablespoons sour cream

6 tablespoons garden fresh salsa

¼ cup chopped fresh cilantro

1. Turn the Instant Pot on the Sauté function. When the pot displays "hot," add the olive oil.

2. Season the steak with the steak seasoning.

3. Add the steak to the pot along with the Worcestershire sauce.

4. Cook each side of the steak for 2 to 3 minutes until the steak turns brown.

5. Remove the steak from the pot and slice thinly.

6. Add the onion to the pot with the remaining olive oil and steak juices and cook until translucent.

7. Remove the onion from the pot.

8. Warm your corn tortillas, then assemble your steak, onion, tomatoes, cheese, sour cream, salsa, and cilantro on top of each.

Philly Cheese Steaks

Michele Ruvola

Makes 6 servings

1 red pepper, sliced

1 green pepper, sliced

1 onion, sliced

2 cloves garlic, minced

2½ pounds thinly sliced steak

1 teaspoon salt

½ teaspoon black pepper

1 (0.7-oz.) package dry Italian dressing mix

1 cup water

1 beef bouillon cube

6 slices provolone cheese

6 hoagie rolls

1. Put all ingredients in the inner pot of the Instant Pot, except the provolone cheese and rolls.

2. Seal the lid, make sure vent is at sealing, and cook for 40 minutes on the Slow Cook setting on low pressure.

3. Let the pressure release naturally for 10 minutes, then do a quick release.

4. Scoop meat and vegetables into rolls.

5. Top with provolone cheese and put on a baking sheet.

6. Broil in oven for 5 minutes.

7. Pour remaining juice in pot into cups for dipping.

Steak Fajitas

Bryan Woolley

Makes 6–8 servings

1 pound New York strip steak

2 tablespoons Worcestershire sauce

1 teaspoon freshly diced garlic

1 green bell pepper

1 red bell pepper

1 yellow bell pepper

1 medium onion

Olive oil for pot

2 cloves garlic, minced

½ cup water

1 cup thinly sliced green cabbage

½ cup chopped cilantro

Juice and zest from 1 lime

¼ cup golden raisins

Salt to taste

Pepper to taste

Flour tortillas

Spice Mix

½ teaspoon seasoned salt

1 teaspoon pepper

½ teaspoon garlic powder

½ teaspoon onion powder

½ teaspoon cumin

½ teaspoon cayenne pepper

1. Cut New York strip steak into thin slices. Place in large bowl. Add Worcestershire sauce and diced garlic; mix together and marinate for 15 minutes.

2. While steak is marinating, clean and slice bell peppers and onion into thin, lengthwise cuts. In a small bowl, whisk the ingredients for the spice mix together and set aside until ready to use.

(Continued on next page)

3. Heat Instant Pot on Sauté mode. Add enough olive oil to lightly coat bottom of pot. When hot, remove New York strip steak from marinade and sauté for about 1 minute.

4. Add sliced bell peppers, onion, spice mix, garlic, water, and ⅓ cup of the marinade.

5. Secure lid and select Steam mode. Steam for 5 minutes. When finished, do a quick release.

6. Remove lid and fold in cabbage, cilantro, lime juice and zest, and raisins. Add salt and pepper to taste.

7. Place fajita mixture on a large platter accompanied by flour tortillas and freshly quartered limes.

Chili Lime Steak and Avocado Bowl

David Murphy

Makes 4–5 servings

1 tablespoon extra-virgin olive oil

1 teaspoon minced garlic

1½–2 pounds fajita steak strips or skirt steak, cut into cubes

1 tablespoon water

2 teaspoons lime juice

½ teaspoon chili powder

½ teaspoon sea salt

½ teaspoon cracked pepper

1 teaspoon Cholula or your favorite hot sauce

2–3 avocados, diced

1. Turn your Instant Pot on Sauté and add olive oil. Once hot, add garlic and cook until a golden color. Then add all remaining ingredients (except avocados), and mix well with wooden spoon.

2. Lock lid, close vent, and cook on Manual at high pressure for 10 minutes.

3. After 10 minutes, do a quick pressure release. Once pressure is released, press Cancel and remove lid.

4. Press Sauté button, and stir the meat to break it up into little chunks.

5. Keep on Sauté mode until liquid has been reduced by half.

6. Allow to cool and serve in a bowl. Surround the meat with your diced avocado.

Bell Pepper Casserole

Janie Steele

Makes 6 servings

1 pound ground beef

1 tablespoon olive oil

3–4 bell peppers, your choice of colors, diced

½ cup diced onions

¾ cup long-grain rice

1 (6-oz.) can diced chilies

1 (14-oz.) can diced tomatoes

1 (24-oz.) jar Ragú or Prego brand marinara sauce

½ teaspoon chili powder

1 teaspoon seasoned salt

2–3 cloves garlic, minced

Serving suggestion:

Serve with cheese: mozzarella, or Parmesan.

1. Using the Sauté function, sauté the beef in the olive oil in inner pot of the Instant Pot.

2. Add in the peppers and onions, then turn the Instant Pot off by hitting the Cancel button.

3. Add the remaining ingredients. Do NOT stir.

4. Secure the lid and make sure vent is at sealing. Turn the Instant Pot on Manual for 10 minutes on high.

5. Let the pressure release naturally.

Cabbage Rolls

Bryan Woolley

Makes 6–8 servings

1 cup water

1 head cabbage

1 cup finely diced carrots

½ cup finely diced onion

½ cup finely diced green onions

2–3 pounds ground beef

1 tablespoon steak seasoning blend

1 tablespoon Worcestershire sauce

1 tablespoon minced garlic

2 cups instant rice

Sauce

2 (14.5 oz) cans crushed tomatoes

1 (14.5 oz) can Italian-style tomato paste

1 tablespoon Italian seasoning herb blend

1 cup water

1. Pour 1 cup of water into Instant Pot and place the steam rack in the pot. Remove core from cabbage and place on steam rack.

2. Steam cook for 5 minutes. Let pressure release naturally.

3. When cabbage is cool enough to handle, remove leaves and set aside.

4. Add carrots, onion, and green onions to a food processor and finely pulse them together.

5. Add carrot mixture to a large bowl along with remaining ingredients (minus cabbage). Mix everything together.

6. Divide meat mixture between prepared cabbage leaves and fold cabbage leaves up like a burrito. Place on steam rack inside Instant Pot.

7. For the sauce, in a separate bowl, mix the crushed tomatoes, tomato paste, Italian seasoning, and 1 cup of water. Pour over the cabbage rolls.

8. Secure lid and pressure cook on high for 8 minutes. Let steam release naturally. Serve with your favorite sides.

One-Pot Spaghetti

Bryan Woolley

Makes 6–8 servings

1 pound spaghetti

1 (24-oz.) jar prepared pasta sauce

1 onion, thinly sliced

2 teaspoons minced garlic

1 pound ground beef

1 teaspoon red pepper flakes

Salt to taste

Pepper to taste

6 cups water

1 cup shredded Parmesan cheese + more to garnish

1. Break spaghetti in half and add to the Instant Pot.

2. Add remaining ingredients except the extra cheese garnish to the Instant Pot (I fill the pasta sauce jar up with water twice and shake it up to remove all the pasta sauce), stirring to combine.

3. Secure lid and pressure cook on high for 10 minutes. Let the pressure release naturally.

4. Remove lid. Fold everything together.

5. Sprinkle with shredded Parmesan cheese.

Spaghetti and Meatballs

Bryan Woolley

Makes 6–8 servings

1 pound ground beef

1 tablespoon minced garlic

1 small red onion, diced

3 tablespoons Italian seasoning herb blend, divided

Olive oil for the pot

1 pound spaghetti, broken in half

12 Roma tomatoes, chopped

1 teaspoon red pepper flakes

1 (6-oz.) can Italian-seasoned tomato paste

6 cups water

Freshly chopped basil

Freshly chopped Italian parsley

Freshly grated Parmesan cheese

Salt to taste

Pepper to taste

Ricotta cheese to garnish

1. In a large bowl, combine beef, garlic, red onion, and 1½ tablespoons Italian seasoning. Mix everything together until combined. Shape into golf ball–sized meatballs and place aside.

2. Heat Instant Pot on Sauté mode. Add enough olive oil to lightly coat bottom of pan. When heated, add meatballs. Do not crowd them. Brown each meatball. If necessary, remove some before adding more, so they aren't crowded while browning. Remove all meatballs when finished.

3. Add the spaghetti, tomatoes, red pepper flakes, tomato paste, and water to the Instant Pot (mix the tomato paste and water together before adding). Sprinkle with remaining Italian seasoning and place the browned meatballs on top.

4. Secure lid on the pot and pressure cook on high for 10 minutes. Allow pressure to release naturally.

5. Once steam has been released, remove lid and sprinkle with basil, parsley, and Parmesan cheese. Gently fold everything together.

6. Serve with your favorite bread on the side. Put a dollop of ricotta cheese on top of each dish. Salt and pepper to taste.

Seafood

Honey Lemon Garlic Salmon

Judy Gascho

Makes 4 servings

5 tablespoons olive oil

3 tablespoons honey

2–3 tablespoons lemon juice

3 cloves garlic, minced

4 fresh salmon filets, 3–4 ounces each

Salt to taste

Pepper to taste

1–2 tablespoons minced parsley, dried or fresh

Lemon slices, optional

1½ cups water

1. Mix olive oil, honey, lemon juice, and minced garlic in a bowl.

2. Place each piece of salmon on a piece of foil big enough to wrap up the piece of fish.

3. Brush each filet generously with the olive oil mixture.

4. Sprinkle with salt, pepper, and parsley flakes.

5. Top each with a thin slice of lemon, if desired.

6. Wrap each filet and seal well at top.

7. Place water in the inner pot of your Instant Pot and place the trivet in the pot. Place wrapped filets on the trivet.

8. Close the lid and turn valve to sealing. Cook on Manual at high pressure for 5 to 8 minutes for smaller pieces, or 10 to 12 minutes if they are large.

9. Carefully release pressure manually at the end of the cooking time.

10. Unwrap and enjoy.

Citrus-Marinated Tilapia

David Murphy

Makes 4 servings

2 tablespoons extra-virgin olive oil

Juice from 1 lemon

Juice from 1 lime

Sea salt to taste

Cracked pepper to taste

4 pieces tilapia

4 FoodSaver bags that have been portioned off for the size of the tilapia, plus a little extra space

1 lemon, sliced into thin wheels

1 lime, sliced into thin wheels

3 cups warm water

1. In a bowl, mix olive oil, lemon juice, lime juice, salt, and pepper. Mix well.

2. Sprinkle each piece of tilapia with a little salt and pepper. Place each one in a bag. Place 1 tablespoon of the citrus mixture into each bag.

3. Top each piece of tilapia with a slice of lemon and lime. Seal each bag—not too tight or liquid will pour out.

4. Add warm water to your pot. Place trivet at the bottom. Then add the 4 bags of sealed tilapia into the water. Lock lid and close vent. Put on Manual at high pressure for 5 minutes. Let pressure naturally release for 5 minutes and then quick release the remaining pressure. Remove bags and allow to cool for a couple of minutes before cutting open and serving.

Salmon Niçoise Salad

Bryan Woolley

Makes 4 servings

¾ cup extra-virgin olive oil

¼ cup rice vinegar

½ teaspoon pepper

½ teaspoon dry mustard

1 teaspoon salt

2 tablespoons lemon juice

1 cup water

2 medium Klondike potatoes, diced into ½-inch pieces

1 pound green beans, snipped

4 salmon fillets

4 eggs, hard-boiled (see recipe on page 2)

1 bunch diced green onions

½ cup capers

4 tomatoes, chopped

12 black olives, pitted

1 tablespoon fresh chopped basil

1. To make the dressing: combine oil, vinegar, pepper, mustard, salt, and lemon juice. Whisk together and set aside.

2. Add steam rack to Instant Pot. Pour in water. Add the potatoes, green beans, and salmon fillets, placing them on top of the steam rack. Be sure to arrange salmon fillets carefully so they are level.

3. Secure lid on the Instant Pot and pressure cook on low for 5 minutes. Allow pressure to release naturally.

4. Remove lid and carefully remove salmon fillets, potatoes, and green beans, and place salmon fillets onto a separate plate. Set aside.

5. Peel and set the eggs aside.

6. Combine potatoes, green beans, green onions, capers, tomatoes, olives, and basil in a large bowl.

7. Drizzle potato mixture with dressing and gently fold everything together. Make sure potatoes are well coated with dressing.

8. Divide potato mixture between four plates. Place a steamed salmon fillet on top of each plate. Slice each hard-boiled egg in half. Place an egg on each plate.

9. Serve the salad with your favorite bread.

White Bean Salad with Skewered Shrimp

Bryan Woolley

Makes 4 servings

2 cups dry great northern beans

16 cups water, divided

24 shrimp, peeled and deveined

Salt to taste

Pepper to taste

2 Roma tomatoes, chopped

1 avocado, diced

½ cup freshly chopped parsley

¼ cup freshly chopped basil

2 tablespoons extra-virgin olive oil

1 tablespoon rice vinegar

1. Rinse uncooked beans. Be sure to pick out any little stones that may be present.

2. Add prepared beans to the Instant Pot along with 8 cups water. Let beans sit for 30 minutes to rehydrate. Drain beans and add another 8 cups clean water to them.

3. Secure lid on Instant Pot and pressure cook beans on high for 10 minutes. Allow pressure to release naturally. Test beans to make sure they are tender; if not, pressure cook for an additional 5 minutes.

4. Place six shrimp on each of four skewers (arrange so the shrimp lay flat on skewer).

5. Salt and pepper shrimp, then grill on both sides until fully cooked. Set aside until ready to use.

6. To make salad, drain and rinse cooked beans in cold water until cooled completely. Place in large bowl along with tomatoes, avocado, parsley, basil, extra-virgin olive oil, and rice vinegar. Gently toss everything together. Don't smash avocado.

7. Salt and pepper to taste.

8. Divide between four plates. Top with grilled shrimp skewers.

Bacon-Wrapped Scallops

Bryan Woolley

Makes 4–6 servings

1½ pounds scallops

1 package bacon

Salt to taste

Pepper to taste

1 cup vegetable stock

¼ cup olive oil

2 cloves garlic, peeled

¼ cup brown sugar

2 limes

1. Wrap each scallop with bacon. Secure with toothpick.

2. Place prepared scallops on baking sheet. Sprinkle with salt and pepper. Set aside until ready to use.

3. Place steam rack in bottom of the Instant Pot. Layer bacon-wrapped scallops on top of each other.

4. Pour vegetable stock into the Instant Pot and secure the lid.

5. Set Instant Pot on Steam and steam for 10 minutes. Allow steam to release naturally.

6. Place olive oil, garlic cloves, and brown sugar in a food processor. Pulse to combine.

7. Remove bacon-wrapped scallops from Instant Pot. Place on baking sheet.

8. Brush each scallop with olive oil mixture. Squeeze juice of one lime over them.

9. Place scallops under broiler for 4 minutes, or until they start to turn golden brown. Turn scallops once while under broiler.

10. Remove scallops from broiler. Squeeze juice from second lime over them. Serve with your favorite sides.

Steamed Broccoli and Salmon

Bryan Woolley

Makes 2 servings

1 cup vegetable stock

2 salmon fillets, 8 ounces each

Salt to taste

Pepper to taste

4 lemon slices

4 stalks fresh thyme

2 cups broccoli florets

½ cucumber, seeded and finely chopped

5 radishes, finely chopped

1 tablespoon soy sauce

1 tablespoon apple cider vinegar

1 tablespoon olive oil

1. Pour vegetable stock into the Instant Pot and add the steam rack.

2. Rinse salmon fillets. Place them on the steam rack. Sprinkle salmon fillets with salt and pepper.

3. Arrange lemon slices and thyme stalks on top of salmon fillets.

4. Place broccoli florets around the two salmon fillets. Secure lid on the Instant Pot, select the Steam mode, and steam for 3 minutes. Let steam release naturally.

5. Combine cucumber and radishes in a small bowl. Add soy sauce, apple cider vinegar, olive oil, salt and pepper to taste. Stir to combine.

6. Serve steamed salmon and broccoli with the cucumber and radish relish.

Steamed Shrimp

Bryan Woolley

Makes 8–10 servings

2 pounds 16/20 shrimps, peeled and thawed

1 cup white wine

¼ cup fresh lemon juice

¼ cup Dijon mustard

¼ cup mayonnaise

1 lemon, sliced, to garnish

1. Clean shrimp by shelling and deveining them. If frozen, thaw by placing the shrimp in a large bowl and running cold water over them for 5 to 10 minutes.

2. Place steam tray into the Instant Pot. Place shrimp on top.

3. Pour white wine and fresh lemon juice into Instant Pot. Secure lid.

4. Select Steam mode and steam for 3 minutes. Let steam release naturally. Remove lid.

5. Place the shrimp in a single layer on a small baking dish. Place in refrigerator to chill.

6. Mix Dijon mustard and mayonnaise together.

7. When shrimp are chilled, serve with Dijon mustard mixture. Garnish with freshly sliced lemon.

Steamed Mussels

Bryan Woolley

Makes 4–6 servings

2 pounds mussels

1 cup white wine

1 cup chicken stock

4 tablespoons butter, melted

⅓ cup freshly chopped chives

½ cup finely chopped parsley

⅓ cup finely chopped red bell pepper

⅓ cup finely chopped onion

1 tablespoon freshly minced garlic

Salt to taste

Pepper to taste

Lemons to garnish

1. Inspect the mussels when purchasing and if any are not tightly sealed, discard them and don't purchase those.

2. Place mussels in large bowl of cold water. Change water every 30 minutes for 2 to 3 hours. Mussels will filter in clean water and discard the dirt inside of them.

3. When mussels have been cleaned, place in the Instant Pot.

4. Pour white wine and chicken stock over mussels. Add melted butter.

5. Add the rest of ingredients except for lemon and, using a large spoon, stir gently to combine.

6. Secure the lid on the Instant Pot and select the Steam mode. Steam for 10 minutes. Allow pressure to release naturally.

7. Remove lid. Any mussel that hasn't opened should be discarded.

8. Heat large sauté pan on the stove. Spray with vegetable oil.

9. Slice lemons into halves. Pan sear the cut side of lemons to caramelize.

10. Serve mussels in shallow bowls with broth. Place pan-seared lemon halves on side.

Vegetables, Grains & Sides

Simple Salted Carrots

Hope Comerford

Makes 4 servings

1 (1-lb.) package baby carrots

1 cup water

1 tablespoon unsalted butter

Sea salt to taste

1. Combine the carrots and water in the inner pot of the Instant Pot.

2. Seal the lid and make sure the vent is on sealing. Select Manual for 2 minutes on high pressure.

3. When cooking time is done, release the pressure manually, then pour the carrots into a strainer.

4. Wipe the inner pot dry. Select the Sauté function and add the butter.

5. When the butter is melted, add the carrots back into the inner pot and sauté them until they are coated well with the butter.

6. Remove the carrots and sprinkle them with the sea salt to taste before serving.

Brown Sugar Glazed Carrots

Michele Ruvola

Makes 10 servings

1 (32-oz.) bag baby carrots
½ cup vegetable broth
½ cup brown sugar
4 tablespoons butter
½ tablespoon salt

1. Place all ingredients in inner pot of the Instant Pot.

2. Secure the lid, turn valve to sealing, and set timer for 4 minutes on Manual at high pressure.

3. When cooking time is up, perform a quick release to release pressure.

4. Stir carrots, then serve.

Smashin' Mashed Carrots

David Murphy

Makes 4 servings

2 pounds baby carrots

1 cup water

2 tablespoons salted butter

2 tablespoons Greek yogurt

1 tablespoon honey

1 tablespoon light brown sugar

1. Add baby carrots and water to pot. Lock lid and close vent. Cook on Manual at high pressure for 4 minutes. Quick release any pressure.

2. Drain water from pot. Add in all remaining ingredients. Use an immersion blender to "mash" your carrots until you get a creamy and velvety texture.

Hash Brown Casserole "Funeral Potatoes"

David Murphy

Makes 6 servings

2 tablespoons unsalted butter + 2 tablespoons, melted

1 small white onion, chopped

4 cloves garlic, minced

½ teaspoon salt

¼ teaspoon black pepper

⅛ teaspoon crushed red pepper flakes

1 cup chicken broth

1 (26-oz.) bag hash browns, shredded and frozen

¾ cup sour cream

2 cups shredded cheddar cheese

1 cup bread crumbs or panko

1. Press Sauté and add 2 tablespoons of unsalted butter.

2. Add the onion and cook it until soft. Add the garlic and Sauté for 30 to 45 seconds.

3. Press Cancel. Add the salt, pepper, and red pepper flakes.

4. Pour in the chicken broth and deglaze the bottom of the pan.

5. Place steamer basket into the pot and pour in frozen hash browns.

6. Lock lid and close the vent. Cook on Manual at high pressure for 2 minutes. Once done, quick release pressure.

7. Remove the hash browns from steamer basket, combine with sour cream and cheese, and stir everything together.

8. Transfer potatoes to an 8-inch greased baking or casserole dish and set it aside.

9. Preheat oven to 400°F. In a medium bowl, add 2 tablespoons of melted butter and panko bread crumbs. Mix well with a fork until mixture is well combined. Scatter breadcrumb mixture across top of potatoes. Place in the oven for approximately 10 to 12 minutes, or until crumb topping is golden brown.

Cheesy Potatoes au Gratin

David Murphy

Makes 6 servings

7 russet potatoes, skin on and sliced ¼-inch thick

1 cup chicken broth

4 ounces cream cheese, room temperature

2 tablespoons heavy cream

1 cup milk

1½ cups sharp cheddar shredded cheese, freshly grated + ½ (reserved) cup

½ cup grated Parmesan cheese

2 cloves garlic, minced

Sea salt to taste

Cracked pepper to taste

1. Place potatoes and chicken broth into your pot. Place on Manual at high pressure for 1 minute.

2. Press Cancel. Carefully remove the potatoes and place them in a greased baking dish.

3. To the remaining chicken broth in your pot, add in all remaining ingredients, except ½ cup reserved cheese. Press Sauté button in Normal mode. Preheat your oven on broil.

4. Stir until you have achieved a creamy and velvety texture, approximately 2 to 3 minutes. Press Cancel. Pour your sauce over the potatoes and then cover with remaining ½ cup cheese.

5. Place baking dish under broiler in oven for approximately 2 minutes, or until you have a beautiful golden-brown crust on top. Allow to cool and serve.

Country-Style Potatoes

Bryan Woolley

Makes 6–8 servings

6 Klondike potatoes, cut into ¼-inch slices

1 teaspoon seasoned salt

2 teaspoons black pepper

1 tablespoon Italian herb seasoning blend

⅓ cup finely minced onion

2 tablespoons olive oil

1 cup vegetable stock

1. Rinse already sliced potatoes.

2. In a large bowl, combine sliced potatoes, seasoned salt, black pepper, Italian seasoning, minced onion, and olive oil. Toss to coat potato slices.

3. Spray one large 32-ounce ramekin or three to four smaller (4-ounce) ramekins with vegetable spray. Fit the prepared potatoes into the ramekins.

4. Place steam rack inside Instant Pot. Pour in vegetable stock. Transfer prepared potatoes into Instant Pot and secure the lid.

5. Pressure cook on high for 6–8 minutes, depending on how large you have cut the potato slices (thicker slices require longer cooking time). I like Klondike variety potatoes, because I don't need to peel them.

6. When pressure cooking is finished, release pressure using quick-release method.

7. Serve with your favorite main dish.

Cheesy Mini Potatoes

Bryan Woolley

Makes 4–6 servings

1 cup chicken stock

1 package Klondike Gourmet Medley Potatoes

1 tablespoon seasoned salt

2 teaspoons black pepper

2 cups finely shredded cheddar cheese

1. Place steam rack inside Instant Pot. Pour in chicken stock.

2. Scrub Klondike Gourmet Medley Potatoes. Place them in the Instant Pot and secure the lid.

3. Pressure cook on high for 5 minutes. Do a quick pressure release.

4. Once pressure is released, remove potatoes and place them on a baking sheet.

5. Using a sharp knife, slice halfway through mini potatoes. Gently press ends toward center of potato to open them.

6. Lightly spray potatoes with vegetable oil spray. Sprinkle with seasoned salt and black pepper.

7. Sprinkle cheese on top of potatoes, gently pressing cheese firmly into the potato slit.

8. Place under broiler until cheese has melted. Serve with your favorite dipping sauce. (I like to serve these as mini appetizers at parties.)

Mashed Potatoes

Colleen Heatwole

Makes 3–4 servings

1 cup water

6 medium-size potatoes, peeled and quartered

2 tablespoons unsalted butter

½–¾ cup milk, warmed

Salt to taste

Pepper to taste

1. Add water to the inner pot of the Instant Pot. Put the steamer basket in the pot and place potatoes in the basket.

2. Seal the lid and make sure vent is at sealing. Using Manual mode, select 5 minutes cook time, high pressure.

3. When cook time ends, do a manual release. Use a fork to test potatoes. If needed, relock lid and cook at high pressure a few minutes more.

4. Transfer potatoes to large mixing bowl. Mash using hand mixer, stirring in butter. Gradually add warmed milk. Season with salt and pepper to taste.

Potatoes with Parsley

Colleen Heatwole

Makes 4 servings

3 tablespoons butter, divided

2 pounds medium red potatoes (about 2 oz. each), halved lengthwise

1 clove garlic, minced

½ teaspoon salt

½ cup chicken broth

2 tablespoons chopped fresh parsley

1. Place 1 tablespoon butter in the inner pot of the Instant Pot and select Sauté.

2. After butter is melted, add potatoes, garlic, and salt, stirring well.

3. Sauté 4 minutes, stirring frequently.

4. Add chicken broth and stir well.

5. Seal lid, make sure vent is on sealing, then select Manual for 5 minutes on high pressure.

6. When cooking time is up, manually release the pressure.

7. Strain potatoes, toss with remaining 2 tablespoons butter and chopped parsley, and serve immediately.

Bacon Ranch Red Potatoes

Hope Comerford

Makes 6 servings

4 strips bacon, chopped into small pieces

2 pounds red potatoes, diced

1 tablespoon fresh chopped parsley

1 teaspoon sea salt

4 cloves garlic, chopped

1 (1-oz.) packet ranch dressing/seasoning mix

⅓ cup water

½ cup shredded sharp white cheddar

2 tablespoons chopped green onions to garnish

1. Set the Instant Pot to Sauté, add the bacon to the inner pot, and cook until crisp.

2. Stir in the potatoes, parsley, sea salt, garlic, ranch dressing seasoning, and water.

3. Secure the lid, make sure vent is at sealing, then set the Instant Pot to Manual for 7 minutes at high pressure.

4. When cooking time is up, do a quick release and carefully open the lid.

5. Stir in the cheese. Garnish with the green onions.

Potato Salad

Bryan Woolley

Makes 6–8 servings

5 russet potatoes

2 cups water, divided

3 carrots, peeled and diced

1 cup chopped broccoli

1 cup fresh or frozen peas

1 cup chopped celery

½ cup chopped green onions

1 cup freshly chopped Italian parsley

1 cup mayonnaise

Salt to taste

Freshly cracked pepper to taste

1. Peel and cut potatoes into ½-inch dice.

2. Place potatoes inside Instant Pot. Add 1 cup of water.

3. Secure lid and pressure cook on high for 5 minutes. Do a quick pressure release. Remove lid.

4. Strain potatoes and place in bowl of cold water to cool.

5. Place carrots and broccoli inside Instant Pot. Add 1 cup of water. Secure lid.

6. Select steam mode and adjust time for 2 minutes. Do a quick pressure release. Remove lid.

7. Strain vegetables. Rinse under cold water to cool.

8. Place cooled potatoes, vegetables, parsley, and mayonnaise in a large bowl.

9. Gently fold together.

10. Add salt and pepper as needed.

11. Cover and place in refrigerator overnight before serving.

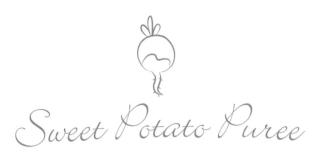

Sweet Potato Puree

Colleen Heatwole

Makes 4–6 servings

3 pounds sweet potatoes, peeled and cut into roughly 2-inch cubes

1 cup water

2 tablespoons butter

1 teaspoon salt

2 teaspoons packed brown sugar

2 teaspoons lemon juice

½ teaspoon cinnamon

⅛ teaspoon nutmeg, optional

1. Place sweet potatoes and water in inner pot of the Instant Pot.

2. Secure the lid, make sure vent is at sealing, then cook for 6 minutes on high using the Manual setting.

3. Manually release the pressure when cook time is up.

4. Drain sweet potatoes and place in large mixing bowl. Mash with potato masher or hand mixer.

5. Once thoroughly mashed, add remaining ingredients.

6. Taste and adjust seasonings to taste.

7. Serve immediately while still hot.

Perfect Sweet Potatoes

Brittney Horst

Makes 4–6 servings

4–6 medium sweet potatoes

1 cup water

1. Scrub skin of sweet potatoes with a brush until clean. Pour water into inner pot of the Instant Pot. Place steamer basket in the bottom of the inner pot. Place sweet potatoes on top of steamer basket.

2. Secure the lid and turn valve to seal.

3. Select the manual mode and set to Pressure Cook on high for 15 minutes.

4. Allow pressure to release naturally (about 10 minutes).

5. Once the pressure valve lowers, remove lid and serve immediately.

Baked Acorn Squash

Dale Peterson

Makes 4 servings

2 small acorn squash, 1¼ pounds each

½ cup cracker crumbs

¼ cup coarsely chopped pecans

2 tablespoons light, soft tub margarine, melted

2 tablespoons brown sugar

Brown sugar substitute to equal 1 tablespoon sugar

¼ teaspoon salt

¼ teaspoon ground nutmeg

2 tablespoons orange juice

1 cup water

1. Cut squash in half. Remove seeds.

2. Combine remaining ingredients. Spoon into squash halves.

3. Place the trivet inside the inner pot of the Instant Pot and pour in water. Place the acorn squash halves on top of the trivet.

4. Secure the lid and set the vent to sealing. Press Manual and set the time for 5 minutes on high pressure.

5. When cook time is up, let the pressure release naturally.

Apple Walnut Squash

Michele Ruvola

Makes 4 servings

1 cup water

2 small acorn squash,
   1¼ pounds each

2 tablespoons brown sugar

Brown sugar substitute to
   equal 1 tablespoon sugar

2 tablespoons light, soft tub
   margarine

3 tablespoons apple juice

1½ teaspoons ground
   cinnamon

¼ teaspoon salt

1 cup toasted walnut halves

1 medium apple, unpeeled,
   chopped

1. Pour water into Instant Pot and place the trivet inside.

2. Cut squash crosswise in half. Remove seeds. Place in the Instant Pot on top of the trivet, cut sides up.

3. Combine brown sugar, brown sugar substitute, margarine, apple juice, cinnamon, and salt. Spoon into squash.

4. Secure the lid and make sure vent is set to sealing. Press Manual and set time for 5 minutes on high pressure.

5. Let the pressure release naturally.

6. Combine walnuts and chopped apple. Add to center of squash when the cook time is over.

Italian Wild Mushrooms

Connie Johnson

Makes 10 servings

2 tablespoons canola oil

2 large onions, chopped

4 cloves garlic, minced

3 large red bell peppers, chopped

3 large green bell peppers, chopped

1 (12-oz.) package oyster mushrooms, cleaned and chopped

3 fresh bay leaves

10 fresh basil leaves, chopped

1 teaspoon salt

1½ teaspoons pepper

1 (28-oz.) can Italian plum tomatoes, crushed or chopped

1. Press Sauté on the Instant Pot and add in the oil. Once the oil is heated, add the onions, garlic, peppers, and mushroom to the oil. Sauté just until mushrooms begin to turn brown.

2. Add remaining ingredients. Stir well.

3. Secure the lid and make sure vent is set to sealing. Press Manual and set time for 3 minutes on high pressure.

4. When cook time is up, release the pressure manually. Discard bay leaves.

Serving suggestion:

Good as an appetizer or on pita bread, or serve over rice or pasta for main dish.

Stewed Tomatoes

Michelle Showalter

Makes 12 servings

2 quarts canned tomatoes

½ cup water

2½ tablespoons sugar

Sugar substitute to equal 1½
   tablespoons sugar

½ teaspoons salt

Dash pepper

2 cups bread cubes

1½ tablespoons light, soft
   tub margarine

1. Place tomatoes in Instant Pot along with the water and sprinkle with sugar, sugar substitute, salt, and pepper.

2. Secure the lid and make sure the vent is set to sealing. Press Manual and set the time for 15 minutes on high pressure.

3. When cook time is up, release the pressure manually.

4. Pour tomatoes into a baking dish.

5. Lightly toast bread cubes in melted margarine. Spread over tomatoes.

6. Bake in oven at 400°F for 8 to 10 minutes.

Corn on the Cob

Hope Comerford

Makes 6 servings

1 cup water

6 small ears of corn, husked and ends cut off

1. Place the trivet in the bottom of the Instant Pot and pour in the water.

2. Place the ears of corn inside.

3. Seal the lid and make sure vent is set to sealing. Press Manual and set time for 2 minutes on high pressure.

4. When cook time is up, release the pressure manually.

Artichokes

Susan Yoder Graber

Makes 4 servings

4 artichokes

1 cup water

2 tablespoons lemon juice

1 teaspoon salt

1. Wash and trim artichokes by cutting off the stems flush with the bottoms of the artichokes and by cutting ¾–1 inch off the tops. Stand upright in the bottom of the inner pot of the Instant Pot.

2. Pour water, lemon juice, and salt over artichokes.

3. Secure the lid and make sure the vent is set to sealing. Press Manual, and set the Instant Pot for 15 minutes for large artichokes, 10 minutes for medium artichokes, or 5 minutes for small artichokes on high pressure.

4. When cook time is up, perform a quick release by releasing the pressure manually.

Serving suggestion:

Pull off individual leaves and dip bottom of each into melted margarine spread. Using your teeth, strip the individual leaf of the meaty portion at the bottom of each leaf. Or, dip the same way into light ranch dressing.

Vegetable Medley

Teena Wagner

Makes 8 servings

2 medium parsnips

4 medium carrots

1 turnip, about 4½ inches diameter

1 cup water

1½ teaspoons salt, divided

3 tablespoons sugar

2 tablespoons canola or olive oil

1. Clean and peel the parsnips, carrots, and turnip. Cut into 1-inch pieces.

2. Place water and 1 teaspoon salt into the Instant Pot's inner pot with the vegetables.

3. Secure the lid and make sure vent is set to sealing. Press Manual and set for 2 minutes on high pressure.

4. When cook time is up, release the pressure manually and press Cancel. Drain the water from the inner pot.

5. Press Sauté and stir in sugar, oil, and ½ teaspoon salt. Cook until sugar is dissolved. Serve.

Vegetable Curry

Sheryl Shenk

Makes 10 servings

1 (16-oz.) package baby carrots

3 medium potatoes, unpeeled, cubed

1 pound fresh or frozen green beans, cut in 2-inch pieces

1 medium green pepper, chopped

1 medium onion, chopped

1–2 cloves garlic, minced

1 (15-oz.) can garbanzo beans, drained

1 (28-oz.) can crushed tomatoes

3 teaspoons curry powder

1½ teaspoons chicken bouillon granules

1¾ cups boiling water

3 tablespoons minute tapioca

1. Combine carrots, potatoes, green beans, pepper, onion, garlic, garbanzo beans, crushed tomatoes, and curry powder in the Instant Pot.

2. Dissolve bouillon in boiling water, then stir in tapioca. Pour over the contents of the Instant Pot and stir.

3. Secure the lid and make sure vent is set to sealing. Press Manual and set for 3 minutes on high pressure.

4. When cook time is up, manually release the pressure.

Serving suggestion:

Serve over cooked brown rice.

Baked Navy Beans

Colleen Heatwole

Makes 8 servings

1 pound navy beans, cleaned and rinsed

10½ cups water, divided

1 tablespoon salt

10 ounces thick sliced bacon (about 8 slices), cut into ½-inch pieces

1 large onion, chopped

½ cup molasses

½ cup ketchup

¼ cup brown sugar

1 teaspoon dry mustard

½ teaspoon salt

¼ teaspoon ground black pepper

1. Soak the navy beans in 8 cups of water that is mixed with salt overnight.
2. Using Sauté function, cook bacon in the inner pot of the Instant Pot until crisp, about 5 minutes, stirring frequently.
3. Remove bacon using slotted spoon and place on plate lined with paper towels.
4. Cook the onion in bacon fat left in the inner pot until tender, about 3 minutes, stirring frequently and scraping up the brown bits on the bottom of the pot as the onion cooks.
5. Add 2½ cups of water, molasses, ketchup, brown sugar, dry mustard, salt, and pepper and stir to combine. Stir in the soaked beans.
6. Secure lid and make sure vent is on sealing. Select Manual at high pressure and set for 25 minutes cook time.
7. When timer on pot beeps, let pressure release naturally for 10 minutes, then do a quick release for the remaining pressure.
8. Discard any beans floating on top. Check beans for tenderness. If not done, pressure cook a few minutes longer.
9. Stir in cooked bacon. Using Slow Cooker function, cook beans uncovered until sauce is desired consistency. Stir frequently to avoid burning the sauce.

Baked Pinto Beans

Janie Steele

Makes 8 servings

1 pound dry pinto beans

1 tablespoon salt

6 cups water

6 slices bacon, diced

1 onion, diced

¾ cup molasses

½ cup brown sugar

1½ teaspoons dry mustard

¾ cup ketchup

½ teaspoon salt

½ teaspoon garlic

1½ teaspoons white wine vinegar

½ teaspoon chili powder

½ teaspoon Worcestershire sauce

1. Put beans, salt, and water in the inner pot of the Instant Pot.

2. Secure the lid and make sure vent is at sealing. Press the Bean/Chili setting and set on normal for 1 hour.

3. Let the pressure release naturally, then drain the beans. Remove the beans from the pot and set aside.

4. Sauté the bacon and onion in inner pot until the bacon is crisp and onion is translucent.

5. Mix seasonings in a bowl.

6. Return beans to pot; stir.

7. Pour seasonings over beans, then stir.

8. Secure the lid and make sure vent is at sealing. Press the Bean/Chili setting and set for 30 minutes.

9. Let pressure release naturally then remove lid. Let sit to thicken.

Best Baked Beans

Carol Eveleth

Makes 8 servings

1 pound dried pinto beans soaked overnight for 8–16 hours

6 cups cold water, divided

Water to fill the pot, room temperature + ½ cup

2 tablespoons butter

1 small onion, diced

2 cloves garlic, finely chopped

1½ teaspoons salt

12 ounces ketchup

1 tablespoon Worcestershire sauce

1 cup brown sugar

½ teaspoon liquid smoke

3 Polish sausages, chopped

1. Overnight Soaking Method: Place dried pinto beans in a large container. Pour 6 cups cold water in the large container and give it a few stirs. Allow beans to soak overnight for 8 to 16 hours. If your house is very warm, place the large container in the fridge to avoid fermentation.

2. Quick Soaking Method: If you're short on time or forgot to soak the beans overnight, you can use this quick soaking method instead. (The result will not be as good as the overnight soaking method.) Place dried pinto beans and 6 cups cold water in the inner pot of the Instant Pot. Close lid, make sure vent is at sealing, and pressure cook on Manual at high pressure for 15 minutes. Let the pressure release naturally.

3. Discard the soaked water and drain the pinto beans through a mesh strainer.

4. Place soaked beans back in the pot and cover with the room temperature water. Close lid, make sure vent is at sealing, and pressure cook on Manual at high pressure for 20 minutes. Let the pressure release naturally for 2 minutes. After 2 minutes, turn the

(Continued on next page)

venting knob to venting position to release the remaining pressure manually. Open the lid carefully.

5. Drain beans. Keep beans in separate bowl.

6. Press Sauté button. Put butter in the inner pot. Add in diced onion and sauté for a minute. Add in chopped garlic cloves and sauté until fragrant (about 30 seconds).

7. Add cooked pinto beans back to the inner pot.

8. Add salt, ketchup, ½ cup of water, Worcestershire sauce, brown sugar, liquid smoke, and chopped Polish sausages to the beans. Mix well. Close lid, make sure vent is at sealing, and cook on Manual at high pressure for 20 minutes. Let the pressure release naturally for 20 minutes. After 20 minutes, turn the venting knob to venting position to release the remaining pressure manually. Open the lid carefully.

Old-Fashioned Ham 'n' Beans

Carolyn Spohn

Makes 8 servings

Meaty ham bone, with as much fat removed as possible (or 2–3 ham hocks)

2 cups great northern beans, sorted and rinsed

2 medium carrots, chopped

1 medium onion, chopped

2 stalks celery, chopped

2 cloves garlic, sliced or minced

4–6 cups broth or water (depending on how "brothy" you want your beans)

Finely chopped onion to garnish, optional

Serving suggestion:

Very good with Jalapeno Corn Bread on page 16.

1. Place all ingredients in the inner pot of the Instant Pot, except for finely chopped onion. Seal the lid, make sure vent is at sealing, and cook on either the Meat or Stew/Soup setting for 30 to 35 minutes on high pressure.

2. Release pressure manually or let it release naturally.

3. Check beans to be sure they are fully cooked. If necessary, pressure cook a while longer, and release pressure as in step 2.

4. Remove ham bone or hocks and trim off the skin, bone, gristle, and visible fat. Return meat to cooker and leave on Keep Warm setting.

5. Serve with chopped onion as a garnish if desired.

Perfect White Rice

Hope Comerford

Makes 4 servings

1 cup uncooked white rice

1 teaspoon grapeseed, olive oil, or coconut oil

1 cup water

Pinch salt

1. Rinse rice under cold running water until the water runs clear, then pour into the inner pot.

2. Add oil, 1 cup of water, and salt to the inner pot.

3. Lock the lid and set the steam valve to its sealing position. Select the Rice button and set to cook for 8 minutes on high pressure.

4. Allow the pressure to release naturally for 10 minutes and then release any remaining pressure manually.

5. Fluff the rice with a fork and serve.

Rice Guiso

Cynthia Hockman-Chupp

Makes 3–6 servings

1 tablespoon oil (I prefer coconut)

1 onion, chopped

1 cup rice

1 teaspoon salt

⅛ teaspoon pepper

¼–½ cup chopped bell pepper, any color or a variety of colors

1–1⅛ cups water

2 tablespoons tomato paste

1. Place all ingredients in inner pot of the Instant Pot. Stir.

2. Secure the lid and make sure vent is at sealing. Push rice button and set for 15 minutes. Allow to cook.

3. Use manual release for a final product that is more moist; natural release for a slightly drier rice.

Perfect Basmati Rice

Carol Eveleth

Makes 3–6 servings

1 cup basmati rice

1 cup water

1. Place basmati rice and water into the inner pot of the Instant Pot. (If you're rinsing the rice, it'll throw off the rice-to-water ratio. So be sure to reduce 3 tablespoons of water from the 1 cup of water stated in the recipe.)

2. Close lid, turn valve to sealing, and cook on Manual at high pressure for 6 minutes. Turn off the heat and do a 10-minute natural release. Release the remaining pressure (if any) and open the lid carefully.

3. Fluff the rice with a rice spatula or fork, then serve with your favorite main dish, or enjoy alone!

Brazilian White Rice

Bryan Woolley

Makes 6 servings

2 tablespoons olive oil

½ cup chopped onion

3 cloves garlic, minced

1 cup chopped carrots, peeled if necessary

2 cups long-grain white rice, rinsed

3¾ cups stock of your choice

1. Heat Instant Pot using Sauté mode. Add olive oil.

2. Add onion, minced garlic, and carrots. Sauté until fragrant (about 3 minutes).

3. Add rinsed rice and sauté with onion mixture until the rice becomes translucent white.

4. Add stock of your choice and secure Instant Pot lid.

5. Choose Rice setting. If Instant Pot doesn't have a Rice setting, pressure cook on low for 12 minutes. Allow pressure to release naturally.

6. Remove lid when pressure has released. Fluff with fork.

Best Brown Rice

Colleen Heatwole

Makes 6–12 servings

2 cups brown rice
2½ cups water

1. Rinse brown rice in a fine mesh strainer.

2. Add rice and water to the inner pot of the Instant Pot.

3. Secure the lid and make sure vent is on sealing.

4. Use Manual setting and select 22 minutes cooking time on high pressure.

5. When cooking time is done, let the pressure release naturally for 10 minutes, then press Cancel and manually release any remaining pressure.

Brown Rice

Marla Folkerts

Makes 4–7 servings

½ cup finely diced onion

2 tablespoons butter

1½ cups brown rice

1¾ cups low-sodium chicken broth

1. Use the Sauté function on the Instant Pot to sauté the diced onion and butter in the inner pot.

2. When the onions are translucent, place everything else in the inner pot.

3. Secure the lid, make sure the vent is at sealing, then use the Manual setting for 22–25 minutes on high pressure.

4. Let the pressure release naturally, then fluff!

Israeli Couscous

Colleen Heatwole

Makes 4–8 servings

2 tablespoons butter

2½ cups chicken broth

1 (16-oz.) package Trader Joe's Harvest Grains Blend couscous (adjust cooking time based on directions if other brand of couscous is used)

Salt to taste

Pepper to taste

1. Melt butter using Sauté function.

2. Add chicken broth and couscous to the Inner Pot. Stir to combine.

3. Lock lid in place, make sure vent is at sealing, then use Manual function and cook on high pressure for 5 minutes. (If substituting a different brand of couscous, cook for one half of the recommended time listed on the package.)

4. When time is up, do a quick release.

5. Fluff with a fork and add salt and pepper to taste.

Parmesan Arborio Rice

Bryan Woolley

Makes 6 servings

2 cups arborio rice

5 cups chicken or vegetable stock

1 cup grated Parmesan cheese

½ cup freshly chopped Italian parsley

Salt to taste

Pepper to taste

1. Pour arborio rice into Instant Pot. Add chicken or vegetable stock. Secure lid and pressure cook on low for 12 minutes.

2. Let pressure release naturally. Remove lid when ready and stir the rice, testing to make sure it's tender. If the rice isn't tender, pressure cook on low for an additional 5 minutes.

3. Stir in Parmesan cheese and parsley.

4. Add salt and pepper as needed.

Quinoa with Almonds and Cranberries

Colleen Heatwole

Makes 4 servings

1 cup quinoa, rinsed well

½ cup roasted slivered almonds

1 bouillon cube, chicken or beef

1½ cups water

¼ teaspoon salt, optional

1 cinnamon stick

½ cup dried cranberries or cherries

1 bay leaf

1. Add all ingredients to the inner pot of the Instant Pot.

2. Secure the lid and make sure vent is on sealing. Cook 2 minutes using high pressure in Manual mode.

3. Turn off pot and let the pressure release naturally for 10 minutes. After 10 minutes are up, release pressure manually.

4. Remove cinnamon stick and bay leaf.

5. Fluff with fork and serve.

Quinoa and Asian Pear Salad

Bryan Woolley

Makes 4–6 servings

1 cup quinoa, rinsed and drained

2⅓ cups water

2 Asian pears, cored, cut into ½-inch pieces

1 cup snow peas, chopped

1 red bell pepper, diced

¼ cup chopped pecans or walnuts, optional

4 green onions, chopped

¼ cup toasted sesame seeds

¼ cup fresh lemon juice

2 tablespoons olive oil

1 teaspoon toasted sesame seed oil

Salt to taste

Pepper to taste

1. Rinse quinoa and place in the Instant Pot. Add water and secure lid.

2. Pressure cook on high for 10 minutes. Let pressure release naturally.

3. Meanwhile, using a large bowl, combine Asian pears, snow peas, bell pepper, pecans or walnuts (if using), green onions, sesame seeds, lemon juice, olive oil, and toasted sesame seed oil. Gently combine everything together and set aside.

4. When pressure has released, transfer quinoa to bowl containing other ingredients. Gently fold everything together and adjust salt and pepper as needed.

5. Chill salad for at least an hour before serving.

Sweet Potato Quinoa Salad

Bryan Woolley

Makes 4–6 servings

1 large sweet potato, peeled and diced into ½-inch pieces

1 cup quinoa, rinsed

2½ cups water

6–8 stalks celery, chopped

1 cup chopped artichoke hearts

1 cup chopped almonds

Juice from 1 large orange

¼ cup olive oil

Salt to taste

Pepper to taste

1. Add sweet potato pieces and quinoa to the Instant Pot. Pour in water. Secure Instant Pot lid.

2. Pressure cook on high for 5 minutes. Let pressure release naturally.

3. Carefully remove lid and strain off any excess water. Let sweet potatoes and quinoa cool completely.

4. In a large bowl, add sweet potatoes, quinoa, chopped celery, artichoke hearts, and almonds. Gently toss to combine everything together.

5. In a separate bowl, whisk the orange juice, olive oil, salt, and pepper together. Pour vinaigrette over the quinoa mixture. Gently toss to combine.

6. Chill and serve.

Tri-Bean Salad

Bryan Woolley

Makes 6–8 servings

1 cup dry cannellini beans or great northern beans

1 cup dry red kidney beans

1 cup dry garbanzo beans

16 cups cold water, divided

1 cup finely chopped celery

1 cup chopped kalamata olives

½ cup diced red onion

1 cup freshly chopped Italian parsley

1 tablespoon freshly chopped dill

1 teaspoon lemon zest

¼ cup cider vinegar

¼ cup sugar

¼ cup vegetable oil

1 tablespoon Dijon mustard

Salt to taste

Pepper to taste

1. Add dry beans along with 8 cups cold water to Instant Pot. Let beans soak for about 30 minutes.

2. Drain water off beans. Add 8 cups cold water back into pot with beans.

3. Secure lid on Instant Pot. Pressure cook on high for 20 minutes. Let pressure release naturally.

4. Once pressure has released, carefully remove lid of Instant Pot and check beans for doneness. If needed, pressure cook for an additional 5 minutes.

5. Once cooked, pour cooked beans into a strainer and run water over them to cool.

6. When beans have cooled, combine all of the beans, celery, kalamata olives, red onion, parsley, dill, and lemon zest into a large bowl.

7. In a separate bowl, whisk together vinegar, sugar, vegetable oil, and Dijon mustard.

8. Add salt and pepper to taste.

9. Pour dressing over beans. Toss to coat. Refrigerate until ready to serve.

Pasta Salad with Corn on the Cob

Bryan Woolley

Makes 6–8 servings

4 cups elbow macaroni

9 cups water, divided

2 cups chopped carrots

1 cup chopped asparagus

1 cup fresh or frozen peas

4 large eggs, hard-boiled
(see recipe on page 2)

2 tablespoons freshly
chopped dill

⅓ cup chopped green onions

¼ cup chopped chives

½ cup diced red bell pepper

1 tablespoon lemon zest

1 cup mayonnaise

1 tablespoon Dijon mustard

2 teaspoons paprika

2 teaspoons dried basil

Salt to taste

Pepper to taste

4 ears corn

1. Add elbow macaroni, 8 cups water, carrots, asparagus, and peas to Instant Pot. Secure lid. Pressure cook on low for 5 minutes. Let steam release naturally.

2. Once steam has released, remove lid and strain pasta mixture under cold water until cool.

3. Peel and chop eggs, and place in a large bowl.

4. To the bowl, add the cooled macaroni mixture, dill, green onions, chives, red bell pepper, lemon zest, mayonnaise, Dijon mustard, paprika, and basil. Gently fold together.

5. Salt and pepper to taste.

6. Place salad in refrigerator until ready to serve.

7. To cook corn on the cob, add corn to the Instant Pot along with 1 cup water. Secure lid and select steam mode. Adjust time for 5 minutes. When finished, allow steam to release naturally.

8. Carefully remove hot corn. Serve with butter, salt, pepper, and the chilled pasta salad.

Pumpkin-Sage Ravioli

Bryan Woolley

Makes 4–6 servings

Pasta Dough

3 cups flour

1 teaspoon salt

4 eggs

2 tablespoons olive oil

Pumpkin Filling

1 cup pumpkin puree

2 teaspoons pumpkin-pie spice

1 teaspoon finely chopped fresh sage

⅓ cup ricotta cheese

1 egg

Salt to taste

Pepper to taste

1 cup water

Sage Butter

4 tablespoons butter

2–3 sage leaves

Cinnamon to garnish

1. To make the pasta dough, add flour and salt together in the bowl of a food processor. Pulse to combine. Change food processor blade to dough blade.

2. Whisk eggs and olive oil together. Gradually pour into flour mixture while machine is running to create a soft dough.

3. Remove dough and divide into 2 parts. Allow dough to rest for 10 minutes.

4. To make the pumpkin filling, in a small bowl add the pumpkin puree, pumpkin pie spice, finely chopped fresh sage, ricotta cheese, and egg. Salt and pepper mixture to your taste, stirring to combine everything. Set aside until ready to use.

5. Roll out each sheet of pasta (¼–⅛-inch thick) and place a small dollop of filling at 2-inch intervals. Place the other sheet of pasta overtop. Press pasta sheet around filling to create the ravioli. Be sure edges are well sealed. Cut into square ravioli shapes and set aside. If you have a favorite ravioli cutter, use it to cut the ravioli.

6. Pour water into the Instant Pot. Spray a bamboo steamer basket with vegetable oil spray. Place the

(Continued on next page)

prepared ravioli onto the prepared bamboo steamer. Set the bamboo steamer into the Instant Pot. Set the Instant Pot to Steam and steam for 5 minutes. Allow steam to release naturally.

7. To make the sage butter, in a large sauté pan, melt 4 tablespoon butter and add 2 to 3 sage leaves.

8. Remove freshly made pumpkin-sage ravioli from the bamboo steamer basket and pan fry them quickly in the sage butter.

9. Serve with a light sprinkling of cinnamon and your favorite sides.

Kid-Friendly Mac & Cheese with Kale

Cynthia Hockman-Chupp

Makes 6–8 servings

1 pound dried elbow macaroni

2 tablespoons butter

½ teaspoon curry powder

½ teaspoon dry mustard powder

1 teaspoon hot pepper sauce

2 teaspoons salt

4 cups water

1 (12-oz.) can evaporated milk

16 ounces shredded cheddar cheese

6 ounces shredded Parmesan cheese

Optional additions

1 tablespoon yellow mustard

1–2 cups frozen chopped kale or spinach, thawed

1. Place first 7 ingredients in the inner pot of the Instant Pot: macaroni, butter, curry power, dry mustard powder, hot pepper sauce, salt, water.

2. Cook on Manual at high pressure for 4 minutes. Quick release the pressure when cooking time ends.

3. Leave pot in Keep Warm mode while you stir in evaporated milk. Then, stir in the cheeses gradually, melting each handful as you go.

4. Optional additions: Add yellow mustard and kale or spinach to finished macaroni and cheese. I usually thaw frozen, chopped kale and add it to the final product.

Desserts & Beverages

Dump Cake

Janie Steele

Makes 8–10 servings

6 tablespoons butter

1 box cake mix (I used spice)

2 (20-oz). cans pie filling (I used apple)

1. Mix butter and dry cake mix in bowl. It will be clumpy.

2. Pour pie filling in the inner pot of the Instant Pot.

3. Pour the dry mix over top.

4. Secure lid and make sure vent is at sealing. Cook for 12 minutes on Manual mode at high pressure.

5. Release pressure manually when cook time is up and remove lid to prevent condensation from getting into cake.

6. Let stand 5 to 10 minutes.

Serving suggestion:

Serve with ice cream.

Carrot Cake

Colleen Heatwole

Makes 10 servings

⅓ cup canola oil

2 eggs

1 tablespoon hot water

½ cup grated raw carrots

¾ cup flour + 2 tablespoons

¾ cup sugar

½ teaspoon baking powder

⅛ teaspoon salt

¼ teaspoon ground allspice

½ teaspoon ground cinnamon

⅛ teaspoon ground cloves

½ cup chopped nuts

½ cup raisins or chopped dates

1 cup water, room temperature

1. In large bowl, beat oil, eggs, and hot water for 1 minute.

2. Add carrots. Mix well.

3. Stir together ¾ cup of flour, sugar, baking powder, salt, allspice, cinnamon, and cloves. Add to creamed mixture.

4. Toss nuts and raisins in bowl with 2 tablespoons of flour. Add to creamed mixture. Mix well.

5. Pour into greased and floured 7-inch springform pan and cover with foil.

6. Place the trivet into your Instant Pot and pour in 1 cup of water. Place a foil sling on top of the trivet, then place the springform pan on top.

7. Secure the lid and make sure lid is set to sealing. Press Steam and set for 50 minutes.

8. When cook time is up, release the pressure manually, then carefully remove the springform pan by using hot pads to lift the pan up by the foil sling. Place on a cooling rack until cool.

Bread Pudding

Winifred Ewy, Helen King, Elaine Patton

Makes 9 servings

8 slices bread (raisin bread is especially good), cubed

3 eggs

2 egg whites

2 cups fat-free half-and-half

2 tablespoons sugar

Sugar substitute to equal 1 tablespoon sugar

½ cup raisins (use only ¼ cup if using raisin bread)

½ teaspoon cinnamon

1½ cups water

Sauce

2 tablespoons light, soft tub margarine

2 tablespoons flour

1 cup water

6 tablespoons sugar

Sugar substitute to equal 3 tablespoons sugar

1 teaspoon vanilla

1. Place bread cubes in a greased 1.6-quart baking dish.

2. Beat together eggs, egg whites, and half-and-half. Stir in sugar, sugar substitute, raisins, and cinnamon. Pour over bread and stir.

3. Cover with foil.

4. Place the trivet into your Instant Pot and pour in 1½ cups of water. Place a foil sling on top of the trivet, then place the baking dish on top.

5. Secure the lid and make sure lid is set to sealing. Press Manual and set time for 30 minutes on high pressure.

6. When cook time is up, let the pressure release naturally for 15 minutes, then release any remaining pressure manually. Carefully remove the springform pan by using hot pads to lift the baking dish out by the foil sling. Let sit for a few minutes, uncovered, while you make the sauce.

7. To make the sauce, melt the margarine in saucepan. Stir in flour until smooth. Gradually add 1 cup of water, sugar, sugar substitute, and vanilla. Bring to a boil. Cook, stirring constantly for 2 minutes, or until thickened.

Serving suggestion:

Serve sauce over warm bread pudding.

Simple Bread Pudding

Melanie L. Thrower

Makes 8 servings

6–8 slices bread, cubed

2 cups fat-free milk

2 eggs

¼ cup sugar

1 teaspoon ground cinnamon

1 teaspoon vanilla

1½ cups water

Sauce

1 tablespoon cornstarch

1 (6-oz.) can concentrated grape juice

1. Place bread cubes in greased 1.6-quart baking dish.

2. Beat together milk and eggs. Stir in sugar, cinnamon, and vanilla. Pour over bread and stir.

3. Cover with foil.

4. Place the trivet into your Instant Pot and pour in water. Place a foil sling on top of the trivet, then place the baking dish on top.

5. Secure the lid and make sure lid is set to sealing. Press Manual and set time for 30 minutes on high pressure.

6. When cook time is up, let the pressure release naturally for 15 minutes, then release any remaining pressure manually. Carefully remove the springform pan by using hot pads to lift the baking dish out by the foil sling. Let sit for a few minutes, uncovered, while you make the sauce.

7. Combine cornstarch and concentrated juice in a saucepan. Heat until boiling, stirring constantly, until sauce is thickened. Serve drizzled over bread pudding.

Apple-Nut Bread Pudding

Ruth Ann Hoover

Makes 10 servings

8 slices raisin bread, cubed

2 medium-sized tart apples, peeled and sliced

1 cup chopped pecans, toasted

½ cup sugar

Sugar substitute to equal ¼ cup sugar

1 teaspoon ground cinnamon

½ teaspoon ground nutmeg

1 egg, lightly beaten

3 egg whites, lightly beaten

2 cups fat-free half-and-half

¼ cup apple juice

2 tablespoons light, soft tub margarine, melted

1½ cup water

1. Place bread cubes, apples, and pecans in greased 1.6-quart baking dish and mix gently.

2. Combine sugar, sugar substitute, cinnamon, and nutmeg. Add remaining ingredients except water. Mix well. Pour over bread mixture.

3. Cover with foil.

4. Place the trivet into your Instant Pot and pour in water. Place a foil sling on top of the trivet, then place the baking dish on top.

5. Secure the lid and make sure lid is set to sealing. Press Manual and set time for 30 minutes on high pressure.

6. When cook time is up, let the pressure release naturally for 15 minutes, then release any remaining pressure manually. Carefully remove the springform pan by using hot pads to lift the baking dish out by the foil sling.

Rice Pudding

Michele Ruvola

Makes 6–8 servings

1 cup arborio rice

1½ cups water

¼ teaspoon salt

2 cups whole milk, divided

½ cup sugar

2 eggs

½ teaspoon vanilla extract

Optional toppings

Cinnamon or toasted coconut and pineapple tidbits for a twist of piña colada rice pudding

1. Place rice, water, and salt into the inner pot of the Instant Pot.

2. Lock lid, make sure vent is at sealing, and select Manual at high pressure and 3 minutes cook time.

3. Let the pressure release naturally for 10 minutes, then manually release the remaining pressure.

4. Add 1½ cups of milk and sugar to rice in pot. Stir to combine.

5. In a bowl, whisk eggs with remaining ½ cup of milk and vanilla extract.

6. Pour through fine mesh strainer into the inner pot of rice to take out any lumps.

7. Select Sauté and cook, stirring constantly so milk does not burn and rice does not stick. Stir until mixture boils. Turn off pot.

8. Serve warm or cold.

9. Top with optional toppings, if desired.

Buttery Rice Pudding

Janie Steele

Makes 6–8 servings

1½ tablespoons butter

1 cup uncooked rice

½ cup sugar

1 cup water

2 cups milk (2% works best)

1 egg

¼ cup evaporated milk

½ teaspoon vanilla extract

½ teaspoon almond extract, optional

Nutmeg, optional

Cinnamon, optional

1. In the inner pot of the Instant Pot, melt butter using the Sauté setting. Add the rice, sugar, water, and milk, then stir.

2. Secure lid and make sure vent is at sealing. Cook on Manual on high pressure for 14 minutes. Let the pressure release naturally when cook time is up.

3. In a bowl whisk together the egg and evaporated milk.

4. Take a spoon of rice mixture and add slowly to egg mixture.

5. Return all to the inner pot and stir in the vanilla and almond extract, if using.

6. Use the Sauté function and bring mixture to bubble for 30 to 60 seconds.

7. Stir slowly so it does not stick to the pot.

8. Use nutmeg or cinnamon to garnish if desired.

Creamy Rice Pudding

Colleen Heatwole

Makes 10 servings

1½ cups arborio rice

2 cups milk, 2% or whole

1 (14-oz.) can coconut milk, light preferred

1 cup water

½ cup granulated sugar

2 teaspoons cinnamon

½ teaspoon salt

1½ teaspoons vanilla extract

1 cup dried tart cherries or golden raisins

1. Rinse rice and drain.

2. Place rice, milk, coconut milk, water, sugar, cinnamon, and salt in the inner pot of the Instant Pot.

3. Select Sauté and bring to boil, stirring constantly to dissolve sugar.

4. As soon as mixture comes to a boil, turn off Sauté.

5. Secure lid and make sure vent is at sealing. Using Manual mode, select 15 minutes on low pressure.

6. When cook time is up, manually release the pressure.

7. Remove lid and add vanilla and dried fruit. Stir.

8. Place cover on pot but do not turn on.

9. Let stand for 15 minutes, then stir and serve.

Lemon Pudding Cake

Jean Butzer

Makes 6 servings

3 eggs, separated

1 teaspoon grated lemon peel

¼ cup lemon juice

1 tablespoon melted light, soft tub margarine

1½ cups fat-free half-and-half

½ cup sugar

Sugar substitute to equal 2 tablespoons sugar

¼ cup flour

⅛ teaspoon salt

1 cup water

1. Beat egg whites until stiff peaks form. Set aside.

2. Beat egg yolks. Blend in lemon peel, lemon juice, margarine, and half-and-half.

3. In separate bowl, combine sugar, sugar substitute, flour, and salt. Add to egg-lemon mixture, beating until smooth.

4. Fold into beaten egg whites.

5. Spoon into a greased and floured 7-inch springform pan. Cover with foil.

6. Place the trivet into your Instant Pot with water. Place a foil sling on top of the trivet, then place the springform pan on top of the trivet.

7. Secure the lid and make sure lid is set to sealing. Press Steam and set time for 40 minutes.

8. Perform a quick release of the pressure when cooking time is done. Remove the springform pan carefully using hot pads with the foil sling and let cool on a cooling rack.

Caramel Apple Pudding Cake

David Murphy

Makes 8 servings

Apple Layer

1 tablespoon unsalted butter

2 Granny Smith apples, peeled, cored, and diced

1 tablespoon sugar

¼ teaspoon nutmeg

¼ teaspoon allspice

¼ teaspoon cinnamon

Pudding Cake

4 cups warm water

1¼ cups all-purpose flour

Pinch salt

2¼ teaspoons baking powder

1 cup plain dry bread crumbs

1 teaspoon cinnamon

½ teaspoon nutmeg

1 stick unsalted butter

½ cup brown sugar

2 large eggs

¼ cup molasses

¼ cup applesauce

Apple Layer

1. Press Sauté on your machine and add butter. Once butter has melted, add in apples and remaining ingredients. Stir frequently. Cook for approximately 5 to 6 minutes. Press Cancel.
2. Spray a 7-cup pudding mold or similar dish with nonstick spray. Add apple topping to the bottom of the mold, and set to the side.

Pudding Cake

1. To your pot, add warm water and trivet. Press Sauté and wait for water to boil. Once boiling, press Cancel.
2. In a medium bowl, add flour, salt, baking powder, bread crumbs, cinnamon, and nutmeg. Mix with a whisk until ingredients are evenly distributed.
3. In a large bowl, cream together butter and brown sugar. Once creamed, add in eggs, molasses, and applesauce. Mix well, but don't overmix. Slowly add in your dry mixture to your wet. Folding works best. Once done, pour batter into mold over the apples.
4. Cover mold with foil and crimp edges to remain sealed. Lock lid and close vent. Cook on Manual at high pressure for 45 minutes. Let pressure naturally release fully (approximately 20 to 25 minutes). Insert a dry toothpick to see if it's done. If not, then cook for an additional 15 to 20 minutes and release pressure naturally. Allow to cool before serving.

Mini Pineapple Upside-Down Cakes

David Murphy

Makes 8

2 cups flour

1 tablespoon baking powder

1 teaspoon salt

½ cup butter, melted + ½ cup, cold and cut into 8 slices

1½ cups sugar

2 eggs

1 teaspoon vanilla

½ cup brown sugar

8 maraschino cherries

1 can crushed pineapple, drained

1½ cups water

1. In a large bowl, mix together the flour, baking powder, salt, ½ cup melted butter, sugar, eggs, and vanilla until smooth.

2. Spray eight 4-ounce ramekins with a light coating of nonstick spray.

3. Add a slice of butter to each ramekin, then sprinkle about 1 teaspoon of brown sugar into bottom of each ramekin, spreading evenly. Then add a cherry in the middle and 1½ tablespoons crushed pineapple around it in each ramekin.

4. Evenly distribute batter to ramekins, on top of the pineapple.

5. Add water to your pot and place trivet in the bottom of the pot. Place ramekins in a pyramid formation onto the trivet—three on the bottom (spaced out), and one in the middle on top of the rims of the other three.

6. Lock the lid and close your vent. Cook on Manual at high pressure for 9 minutes. Once done, quick release the pressure. Allow a few minutes to cool, and carefully remove the ramekins with tongs.

7. While the first batch is cooling, add your second batch to the Instant Pot. When ready to serve, simply turn upside down onto a plate.

Pea Picker's Cake

David Murphy

Makes 8 mini cakes

Topping

16 ounces Cool Whip topping

1 (20-oz.) can pineapple, crushed and drained, reserving the juice

1 (3-oz.) box instant vanilla pudding

Cake

2 cups flour

1 tablespoon baking powder

1 teaspoon salt

½ cup melted butter

1½ cups sugar

2 eggs

1 teaspoon vanilla extract

1 (15-oz.) can mandarin orange segments + juice from the can

1 cup water

1. In one bowl, combine the topping ingredients together. Cover and place in the fridge.

2. To make the cake, in a large bowl, mix together the flour, baking powder, salt, melted butter, sugar, eggs, and vanilla until smooth.

3. Remove 8 mandarin segments and set to the side. Add the remaining mandarin oranges plus the juice into the batter. Mix well.

4. Lightly coat eight 4-ounce ramekins with the nonstick spray. Evenly distribute batter to ramekins.

5. Place water in your pot and place trivet at the bottom of the pot. Place ramekins in a pyramid formation onto the trivet—three on the bottom (spaced out), and one in the middle on top of the rims of the other three.

6. Lock lid and close vent. Cook on Manual at high pressure for 9 minutes, and then quick release pressure once done.

7. Remove and allow to cool on a baker's rack. While cooling, work on your second batch. Allow ramekins to cool for 10 minutes, and then place in the fridge for 1 hour.

8. Remove cakes from ramekins. Cover with topping and garnish with a mandarin orange segment.

Dampfnudel

David Murphy

Makes 1 dozen

1½ teaspoons active dry
  yeast

2 tablespoons sugar, divided

¼ cup lukewarm water

¾ cup lukewarm milk

Pinch sea salt

2 tablespoons melted butter

2½ cups all-purpose flour,
  sifted

1½ cups warm water

Vanilla sauce or sweetened
  condensed milk for
  topping, optional

1. Dissolve the yeast and 1 tablespoon sugar in warm water. Let the mixture stand until bubbly. In another bowl, add 1 tablespoon sugar, lukewarm milk, salt, and melted butter. Mix until sugar has been dissolved.

2. Add the yeast mixture to the milk mixture and then add the flour and knead until dough is smooth and elastic (approximately 7 to 8 minutes). Add flour as necessary, until the dough can be formed into a soft ball.

3. Lightly spray a bowl with nonstick spray and place the dough in it. Allow the dough to double in size. This will take about 1 hour.

4. Once done, punch dough. Remove from bowl and knead for 2 minutes on a lightly floured surface. Divide dough into 12 equal pieces and roll them into balls. Place them in an Instant Pot steamer basket. Side by side is fine; they will all fit. Allow dough balls to rise for about 10 to 15 minutes.

5. Place warm water into your pot and place trivet into bottom. Place steamer basket on trivet. Close lid and lock vent. Cook on Manual at high pressure for 40 minutes and let pressure naturally release. Serve warm or chilled with sauce of your choice.

Philippine Steamed Cake (Puto)

David Murphy

Makes 8 servings

¼ teaspoon salt

1¾ cups all-purpose flour

1 cup sugar

2 tablespoons baking powder

¼ teaspoon salt

2 large egg whites

¼ cup milk

3½ cups water, divided

1. In a large bowl, add all dry ingredients and whisk together. In another bowl, add egg whites, milk, and 1½ cups of water. With a handheld mixer, beat on medium speed for about 5 to 6 minutes.

2. Add the wet ingredients to the dry and mix well. Lightly spray a 7-cup mold with nonstick spray. Pour batter into mold and cover with foil.

3. Add 2 cups of water into your pot and insert trivet. Place mold onto trivet. Cook on Manual at high pressure for 40 minutes and let pressure naturally release for 10 minutes. Be sure to quick release any remaining pressure.

Sticky Toffee Cake

David Murphy

Makes 4

4 tablespoons butter, softened

¾ cup sugar

1 large egg, lightly beaten

1½ cups all-purpose flour

1 teaspoon baking powder

1¼ cups pitted dates, chopped finely

1 teaspoon baking soda

1 teaspoon vanilla extract

1 cup boiling water

1½ cups water, room temperature

Caramel sauce for serving

1. In a bowl, cream together butter and sugar until fluffy peaks have formed. Add egg and lightly mix. Slowly add in flour and baking powder—your mixture will look very crumbly at this moment.

2. In a separate bowl, add dates, baking soda, vanilla extract, and 1 cup of boiling water. Mix well. Add this mixture to your other bowl of dough, and incorporate.

3. Lightly spray eight 4-ounce ramekins with nonstick spray. Distribute dough into ramekins, filling ¾ of the way. Cover each ramekin with foil.

4. Add 1½ cups of water to your pot and insert trivet. Place ramekins on trivet. Don't be afraid to stack! Lock lid and close vent. Cook on Manual on high pressure for 30 minutes and let pressure naturally release for 10 minutes. Quick release any remaining pressure.

5. Carefully remove ramekins from your pot. Allow to cool, and then flip onto a plate upside down. Remove ramekin. Serve with your favorite caramel sauce.

Steamed Gingerbread

Bryan Woolley

Makes 8–10 servings

½ cup butter, softened

¼ cup sugar

¼ cup brown sugar

1 large egg

2 cups flour

2 teaspoons baking powder

½ teaspoon baking soda

¼ teaspoon salt

1 tablespoon ground ginger

2 teaspoons cinnamon

⅔ cup milk

⅔ cup molasses

1 cup water

Fresh cream for serving

1. In the bowl of your stand mixer, using the paddle attachment, cream the butter and sugars together for 3 minutes. Once butter and sugars are creamed, add egg. Blend thoroughly.

2. In a separate bowl, combine flour, baking powder, baking soda, salt, ginger, and cinnamon. Whisk together to fully combine. Set aside until ready to use.

3. Measure milk and molasses together; set aside. (I heat the milk and molasses mixture to help them combine easier.)

4. Add dry and wet ingredients (alternating) into the butter mixture until everything is fully incorporated.

5. Spray the inside of a 32-ounce ramekin with vegetable spray. Pour batter into the prepared ramekin. Place the rack into the Instant Pot and pour water into the bottom of the pot. Place the ramekin on top of the rack. Set it to Cake mode. When finished, let steam release naturally. Remove lid.

6. Serve with fresh cream and enjoy!

Cheesecake in a Jar

Bryan Woolley

Makes 4–5 servings

1 cup sliced strawberries

1 cup raspberries

1 cup blueberries

1 cup blackberries

4 tablespoons apricot jam

2 (8-oz.) packages cream cheese

5 eggs

¼ cup sour cream

⅔ cup milk

¼ cup cornstarch

1 teaspoon almond extract

1 teaspoon vanilla extract

2 cups graham cracker crumbs

1 cup water

1. Combine berries in a large bowl. Fold apricot jam into them (it's easier if you warm the jam first). Set aside until ready to use.

2. In a food processor, combine cream cheese, eggs, sour cream, milk, cornstarch, and almond and vanilla extracts; puree until smooth.

3. Gather 4 to 5 widemouthed 8-ounce jelly jars; press ½ inch of graham cracker crumbs into bottom of each. Reserve extra crumbs.

4. Divide and pour the cheesecake batter into each jar, filling ¾ of the way.

5. Place steam rack in bottom of Instant Pot. Pour water into the pot.

6. Place prepared cheesecake jars onto the steam rack.

7. Pressure cook on low for 25 minutes. Let steam release naturally. Remove Instant Pot lid. Allow mini-cheesecakes to fully cool.

8. Sprinkle tops with extra graham cracker crumbs. Top with fresh berries mixture.

Cookies & Cream Cheesecake (Gluten-Free)

Hope Comerford

Makes 6 servings

Crust

12 whole gluten-free chocolate sandwich cookies, crushed into crumbs

2 tablespoons salted butter, melted

Cheesecake

16 ounces cream cheese, room temperature

½ cup granulated sugar

2 large eggs, room temperature

1 tablespoon gluten-free all-purpose flour

¼ cup heavy cream

2 teaspoons pure vanilla extract

8 whole gluten-free chocolate sandwich cookies, coarsely chopped

1½ cups water

Toppings

1 cup whipping cream, whipped

8 whole gluten-free chocolate sandwich cookies, coarsely chopped

Chocolate sauce, optional

1. Tightly wrap the bottom of 7-inch springform pan in foil. Spray the inside with nonstick cooking spray.

2. To make the crust, in a small bowl, stir together crushed gluten-free chocolate sandwich cookies and melted butter. Press the crumbs into the bottom of the prepared pan (the bottom of a glass cup is a great tool for this). Place this in the freezer for 10 to 15 minutes.

(Continued on next page)

3. To make the cheesecake, in a large bowl, beat the cream cheese until smooth. (You can use an electric mixer, or stand mixer with paddle attachment.)

4. Add the sugar and mix until combined.

5. Add the eggs, one at a time, making sure each is fully incorporated before adding the next. Be sure to scrape down the bowl in between each egg.

6. Add in the flour, heavy cream, and vanilla and continue to mix until smooth.

7. Gently fold in the 8 chopped gluten-free chocolate sandwich cookies and pour this batter into the pan you had in the freezer. Cover the top of the pan with a piece of foil.

8. Pour water into the inner pot and place the trivet in the bottom of the pot.

9. Create a foil sling by folding a 20-inch long piece of foil in half lengthwise two times. This sling will allow you to easily place and remove the springform pan from the pot.

10. Place the cheesecake pan in the center of the sling and carefully lower the pan into the inner pot. Fold down the excess foil from the sling to ensure the pot closes properly.

11. Lock the lid into place and make sure the vent is at sealing. Press the Manual button and cook on high pressure for 35 minutes.

12. When the Instant Pot beeps, hit the Keep Warm/Cancel button to turn off the pressure cooker. Allow the pressure to release naturally for 10 minutes and then do a quick release to release any pressure remaining in the pot.

13. Carefully remove the lid. Gently unfold the foil sling and remove the cheesecake from the pot to a cooling rack using the foil sling "handles." Uncover the cheesecake and allow it to cool to room temperature.

14. Once the cheesecake has cooled, refrigerate it for at least 8 hours, or overnight.

15. Before serving, top with whipped cream, chopped gluten-free chocolate sandwich cookies, and a drizzle of chocolate sauce if desired.

Creamy Orange Cheesecake

Jeanette Oberholtzer

Makes 10 servings

Crust

¾ cup graham cracker crumbs

2 tablespoons sugar

3 tablespoons melted, light, soft tub margarine

Filling

2 (8-oz.) packages fat-free cream cheese, room temperature

⅔ cup sugar

2 eggs

1 egg yolk

¼ cup frozen orange juice concentrate

1 teaspoon orange zest

1 tablespoon flour

½ teaspoon vanilla

1½ cups water

1. Combine crust ingredients. Pat into 7-inch springform pan.

2. To make filling, cream together cream cheese and sugar. Add eggs and yolk. Beat for 3 minutes.

3. Beat in juice, zest, flour, and vanilla. Beat 2 minutes.

4. Pour batter into crust. Cover with foil.

5. Place the trivet into your Instant Pot and pour in water. Place a foil sling on top of the trivet, then place the springform pan on top.

6. Secure the lid and make sure lid is set to sealing. Press Manual and set for 35 minutes on high pressure.

7. When cook time is up, press Cancel and allow the pressure to release naturally for 7 minutes, then release the remaining pressure manually.

8. Carefully remove the springform pan by using hot pads to lift the pan up by the foil sling. Uncover and place on a cooling rack until cool, then refrigerate for 8 hours.

Serving suggestion:

Serve with thawed frozen whipped topping and fresh or mandarin orange slices.

Cherry Delight

Anna Musser, Marianne J. Troyer

Makes 12 servings

1 (20-oz.) can cherry pie
filling, light

½ package yellow cake mix

¼ cup light, soft tub
margarine, melted

⅓ cup walnuts, optional

1 cup water

1. Grease a 7-inch springform pan then pour the pie filing inside.

2. Combine dry cake mix and margarine (mixture will be crumbly) in a bowl. Sprinkle over filling. Sprinkle with walnuts.

3. Cover the pan with foil.

4. Place the trivet into your Instant Pot and pour in water. Place a foil sling on top of the trivet, then place the springform pan on top.

5. Secure the lid and make sure lid is set to sealing. Press Steam and set for 50 minutes.

6. When cook time is up, release the pressure manually, then carefully remove the springform pan by using hot pads to lift the pan up by the foil sling. Place on a cooling rack for 1 to 2 hours.

Serving suggestion:

Serve in bowls with dips of ice cream.

Black and Blue Cobbler

Renee Shirk

Makes 12 servings

1 cup flour

12 tablespoons sugar, divided

Sugar substitute to equal 6 tablespoons sugar, divided

1 teaspoon baking powder

¼ teaspoon salt

¼ teaspoon ground cinnamon

¼ teaspoon ground nutmeg

2 eggs, beaten

2 tablespoons milk

2 tablespoons vegetable oil

2 cups blueberries, fresh or frozen

2 cups blackberries, fresh or frozen

1¾ cup water

1 teaspoon grated orange peel

Whipped topping or ice cream, optional

1. Combine flour, 6 tablespoon sugar, sugar substitute equal to 3 tablespoons sugar, baking powder, salt, cinnamon, and nutmeg.

2. Combine eggs, milk, and oil. Stir into dry ingredients until moistened.

3. Spread the batter evenly over bottom of greased 1½-quart baking dish.

4. In a saucepan, combine berries, water, orange peel, 6 tablespoons sugar, and sugar substitute equal to 3 tablespoons sugar. Bring to boil. Remove from heat and pour over batter. Cover with foil.

5. Place the trivet into your Instant Pot and pour in water. Place a foil sling on top of the trivet, then place the baking dish on top.

6. Secure the lid and make sure lid is set to sealing. Press Manual and set for 35 minutes on high pressure.

7. When cook time is up, allow the pressure to release naturally for 10 minutes, then release the remaining pressure manually. Carefully remove the baking dish by using hot pads to lift the foil sling. Place on a cooling rack, uncovered for 30 minutes.

Serving suggestion:

Serve with whipped topping or ice cream, if desired.

Coconut Cherry Cobbler

Bryan Woolley

Makes 10–12 servings

3 cups flour

1½ cups sugar, divided

1 teaspoon salt

2 teaspoons baking powder

1½ cups coconut milk

2 eggs

1 tablespoon vanilla extract

¼ cup olive oil

4 tablespoons butter

1 cup sugar

4 cups fresh pie cherries, pitted

1. In medium bowl, add flour, ½ cup sugar, salt, and baking powder, whisking everything together to combine. Set aside.

2. In another bowl, combine coconut milk, eggs, vanilla, and olive oil. Whisk together to combine.

3. Add coconut milk mixture to flour mixture. Stir to combine. If necessary, use additional coconut milk to create a thick pancake-like batter. Set aside.

4. Select Sauté mode on the Instant Pot.

5. Add butter and melt while gently stirring. Once butter is melted, add 1 cup sugar. Mix together.

6. Add freshly pitted pie cherries to the butter and sugar. Sauté for 2 to 3 minutes.

7. Pour cobbler batter over cherries. Secure Instant Pot. Set mode to Cake.

8. When finished, let pressure release naturally. Remove lid.

9. Serve warm with your favorite ice cream.

Chocolate Pots de Crème

Judy Gascho

Makes 6–7 servings

1½ cups heavy cream

½ cup whole milk

8 oz. unsweetened baking chocolate

5 large egg yolks

¼ cup sugar

Pinch salt

1½ cups water

Whipped cream and grated chocolate to garnish, optional

1. In a small saucepan, bring the cream and milk to a simmer.
2. Melt chocolate at 50% power in 30-second increments in microwave, stirring after each increment.
3. In a large mixing bowl, whisk together egg yolks, sugar, and salt. Slowly whisk in hot cream and milk. Whisk in melted chocolate until blended.
4. Pour into 6 to 7 custard cups. Wrap each tightly with foil.
5. Add water to the inner pot of the Instant Pot and place the trivet in the bottom.
6. Place 3 to 4 wrapped cups on the trivet. Place a second trivet on top of the cups and place the remaining cups on the second trivet. (If you don't have a second trivet, place the remaining cups staggered on the top of the bottom layer of cups.)
7. Lock the lid in place and make sure vent is at sealing. Select high pressure in Manual mode and set the timer for 6 minutes. When cooking time is up, turn off the pressure cooker and let the pressure release for 15 minutes naturally, then do a quick pressure release to release any remaining pressure. When the valve drops, carefully remove lid.
8. Carefully remove the cups to a wire rack and remove foil immediately. Cool.
9. When cool, refrigerate cups covered with plastic wrap for at least 4 hours or overnight.

Chocolate Tofu Surprise

David Murphy

Makes 1 tart, or 12 minis

Crust

1¼ cups water

1½ cups semisweet chocolate chips

6 tablespoons granulated sugar

6 tablespoons unsweetened cocoa

1 tablespoon vanilla extract

¾ cup couscous

Tofu Filling

½ cup sugar

2 cups semisweet chocolate chips

2 tablespoons water, as needed

19 ounces silken tofu, drained well

½ cup unsweetened cocoa powder

Crust

1. To your pot, add water, chocolate chips, sugar, cocoa, and vanilla extract. Press Sauté and bring ingredients to a simmer. During the process, stir until the chocolate chips have melted and it has started to thicken a little.

2. Once the thickening process has started, press the Cancel button on your pot. Stir in the couscous. Let it rest in the mixture for 2 to 3 minutes, and then remove the pot from the machine. Allow to cool for 15 to 20 minutes. Spread the crust evenly into the bottom of a 9-inch springform pan. Clean and dry your pot for next portion of recipe.

Tofu Filling

1. Press Sauté button at Low Heat setting on your machine. Add sugar, chocolate chips, and 1 tablespoon or more of water as needed. Stir constantly to ensure that you get a smooth mixture.

2. Once you've achieved the smooth mixture, remove pot from machine. To a blender or food processor, add chocolate mixture, tofu, and cocoa powder. Blend until completely smooth. Pour your tofu filling into the crust-lined pan. Cover and place in the fridge for at least 2 hours before serving. Overnight works best.

Monkey Bread

David Murphy

Makes 4 mini loves

½ cup sugar

1½ teaspoons cinnamon

1 can Pillsbury Grands! Southern Homestyle Butter Tastin' biscuits

½ stick butter

½ cup light brown sugar

1 cup water

1. In a large bowl or plastic bag, add sugar and cinnamon. Combine well.

2. Cut 4 biscuits in quarters, add to sugar mixture, and coat thoroughly. Place sugar-coated biscuit pieces into 2 mini loaf pans. Repeat the process until your biscuits are used or your pan is full.

3. Add butter and brown sugar into a small bowl, and place in the microwave for 45 seconds. Once butter is melted, stir thoroughly with a fork. Evenly distribute the caramel sauce between the two loaf pans.

4. Add water to your pot and place trivet into the bottom. Place both loaf pans onto trivet, and lightly cover the top of the loaf pans with a piece of foil.

5. Place on Manual at high pressure for 21 minutes, and natural pressure release for 5 minutes then quick pressure release.

Potato Candy

David Murphy

Makes approximately 3 dozen pieces

1 small russet potato, peeled and sliced

1 cup water

8 cups powdered sugar

⅔ cup peanut butter

1. Place potato in pot and add water. Close lid and lock vent. Cook on Manual at high pressure for 5 minutes. Quick release pressure once done.

2. Drain potato and place in a medium bowl. Use a hand mixer to beat the potato until it is lump-free.

3. Slowly add in all powdered sugar. Once done, place on a large piece of waxed paper lightly coated with powdered sugar.

4. Roll potato mixture out into a ¼-inch thick rectangular shape. Spread the peanut butter evenly on top. Starting at a long side, roll as if you were making cinnamon rolls.

5. Place in the fridge for about 1 hour. Remove wax paper and cut into pinwheel slices.

Steamed and Raisin Yogurt "Cookies"

David Murphy

Makes 1 dozen

2½ tablespoons granulated sugar

1 cup self-rising flour

2 tablespoons vegetable oil

½ cup Greek yogurt

¼ cup raisins

1½ cups warm water

1. In a bowl, whisk together sugar and flour. Add in oil and yogurt. Mix well with a fork. Gently fold in raisins.

2. Cut parchment paper into 3 x 3-inch squares. Add about 1 tablespoon of dough to each piece of parchment paper.

3. Add warm water to your pot. Insert trivet.

4. Place 4 raisin "cookies" in your authentic Instant Pot silicone steamer basket. Place basket on trivet. Lock lid and close vent. Cook on Manual at high pressure for 10 minutes and allow to natural pressure release for 10. Quick release any remaining pressure.

5. Remove steamer basket and allow "cookies" to cool.

Sweet Sticky Rice with Mango

Bryan Woolley

Makes 6–8 servings

Coconut Sauce

2 cups coconut milk

½ cup sugar

½ teaspoon salt

1 tablespoon rice flour

Sweet Sticky Rice

2 cups sweet rice

3 cups water

3 cups coconut milk

¾ cup sugar

½ teaspoon salt

3–4 ripe mangoes to garnish

1. To make the sauce, add coconut milk, sugar, salt, and rice flour to Instant Pot and select the Sauté mode.

2. Bring to boil while gently stirring. Let mixture thicken. Remove sauce from the Instant Pot and set aside.

3. To make the rice, add the sweet rice and water to the Instant Pot. Select Rice mode.

4. Once rice is cooked, remove the lid and add coconut milk, sugar, and salt to cooked rice. Secure the lid and steam for 5 minutes. Let the steam release naturally before removing the lid.

5. Peel and slice fresh mango to serve on side.

6. To serve, place a large spoonful of sweet sticky rice on plate with some fresh mango on the side. Drizzle with the coconut sauce.

Quick Yummy Peaches

Willard E. Roth

Makes 8 servings

⅓ cup buttermilk baking mix

⅔ cup dry quick oats

¼ cup brown sugar

Brown sugar substitute to
equal 2 tablespoons sugar

1 teaspoon cinnamon

4 cups sliced peaches,
canned or fresh

½ cup peach juice or water

1 cup water

1. Mix together baking mix, oats, brown sugar, brown sugar substitute, and cinnamon. Mix in the peaches and peach juice.

2. Pour mixture into a 1.6-quart baking dish. Cover with foil.

3. Place the trivet into your Instant Pot and pour in water. Place a foil sling on top of the trivet, then place the baking dish on top.

4. Secure the lid and make sure lid is set to sealing. Press Manual and set for 10 minutes on high pressure.

5. When cook time is up, let the pressure release naturally for 10 minutes, then release any remaining pressure manually. Carefully remove the baking dish by using hot pads to lift the foil sling. Uncover and let cool for about 20 to 30 minutes.

Instant Pot Tapioca

Nancy W. Huber

Makes 6 servings

2 cups water

1 cup small pearl tapioca

4 eggs

½ cup evaporated skim milk

½ cup sugar

Sugar substitute to equal ¼ cup sugar

1 teaspoon vanilla

Fruit of choice, optional

1. Combine water and tapioca in Instant Pot.

2. Secure lid and make sure vent is set to sealing. Press Manual and set for 5 minutes on high pressure.

3. Perform a quick release. Press Cancel, remove lid, and press Sauté.

4. Whisk together eggs and evaporated milk. Very slowly add to the Instant Pot, stirring constantly so the eggs don't scramble.

5. Stir in the sugar substitute until it's dissolved, press Cancel, then stir in the vanilla.

6. Allow to cool thoroughly, then refrigerate at least 4 hours.

Serving suggestion:

Serve with fruit.

Wine-Poached Pears

Hope Comerford

Makes 6 servings

1 bottle red blend wine

1 cup Truvia brown sugar blend

1 teaspoon grated lemon peel

6 fresh pears, peeled, but stem attached

2 cinnamon sticks

1. In the Instant Pot, mix together the wine, brown sugar blend, and lemon peel.

2. Place the pears and cinnamon sticks into the liquid inside the Instant Pot.

3. Secure the lid and make sure the vent is set to sealing. Press Manual and set time for 5 minutes on high pressure.

4. Let the pressure release naturally for 10 minutes, then perform a quick release.

5. Remove the lid and carefully remove the pears with tongs and set aside.

6. Press Sauté and continue to cook until the sauce has reduced to a third of the original amount.

Serving suggestion:

Serve pears at room temperature or chilled with the sauce drizzled over the top.

Scalloped Pineapples

Shirley Hinh

Makes 8 servings

½ cup sugar

Sugar substitute to equal
¼ cup sugar

3 eggs

¼ cup light, soft margarine,
melted

¾ cup milk

1 (20-oz.) can crushed
pineapple, drained

8 slices bread, crusts
removed and cubed

1. Mix together all ingredients in the Instant Pot.

2. Secure the lid and set to Slow Cook mode on high for
2 hours. Reduce heat to low and cook 1 more hour.

Baked Apples

Judy Gascho

Makes 6 servings

6 medium apples, cored

1 cup apple juice or cider

¼ cup raisins or dried cranberries

½ cup brown sugar

1 teaspoon cinnamon

1. Put the apples into the inner pot of the Instant Pot.

2. Pour in the apple juice or cider. Sprinkle the raisins, brown sugar, and cinnamon over the apples.

3. Close and lock the lid and be sure the steam vent is in the sealing position.

4. Cook for 9 minutes on Manual mode at high pressure.

5. When time is up, unplug and turn off the pressure cooker. Let pressure release naturally for 15 minutes, then manually release any remaining pressure.

6. Take off lid and remove apples to individual small bowls, adding cooking liquid to each.

Aunt Minnie's Applesauce with Sweet Dumplings

Bryan Woolley

Makes 6–8 servings

10–12 apples (I like McIntosh or Golden Delicious)

1 tablespoon cinnamon

1 teaspoon nutmeg

2–3 cups sugar (or more for a sweeter applesauce)

½ cup water

½ teaspoon salt

Dumpling

2 cups all-purpose flour

1 tablespoon baking powder

4 tablespoon cold butter

½ cup sugar

1 cup milk (or more if needed)

1 cup water

1. Peel and core apples. Slice into wedges and place into the Instant Pot. Add cinnamon, nutmeg, sugar, ½ cup of water, and salt. Stir to combine.

2. Secure Instant Pot lid. Pressure cook on high for 5 minutes. Let pressure release naturally. Remove lid.

3. Using a potato masher, mash cooked apples into a sauce.

4. Using a food processor, add flour, baking powder, butter, and sugar. Pulse together until butter is cut into flour, and mixture resembles coarse cornmeal.

5. Transfer flour mixture into mixing bowl. Add milk.

6. Using a fork, gently mix milk and flour mixture together until it combines into a wet dough. If needed, add more milk to achieve a wet dough.

7. Add 1 cup of water to applesauce and stir together. Spoon-drop prepared dumplings on top of the applesauce.

8. Secure Instant Pot lid. Select Steam mode and steam for 5 minutes. Let pressure release naturally. Remove lid.

9. Spoon dumplings and applesauce into small bowl. Pour some cream over the top and enjoy!

Sweetened Dumplings with Rhubarb and Fresh Cream

Bryan Woolley

Makes 6–8 servings

4 cups cleaned and sliced rhubarb stalks

1½ cups sugar, divided

Zest and juice from 1 orange

Zest and juice from 1 lemon

2 cups flour

2 eggs

½ cup cream + more for serving

1 teaspoon vanilla extract

¼ teaspoon baking powder

½ teaspoon salt

Cinnamon, nutmeg, and sugar for sprinkling

1. Select Sauté on the Instant Pot.

2. Add rhubarb, 1 cup sugar, and juice and zest from the orange and lemon to the pot.

3. Stir everything together. Bring to boil. Cook until rhubarb is soft and pulpy (about 20 minutes).

4. Combine flour, eggs, ½ cup cream, ½ cup sugar, vanilla, baking powder, and salt in a large bowl. Mix together.

5. Drop dough a spoonful at a time on top of rhubarb. Sprinkle top of dumplings with cinnamon, nutmeg, and sugar.

6. Secure lid. Steam for 10 minutes. Let steam release naturally.

7. Serve rhubarb and dumplings warm with fresh cream poured over top.

Cider

Anita Troyer

Makes 6–8 servings

7 medium Gala or Honeycrisp apples

2 pears

1 orange

3 cinnamon sticks

1 teaspoon whole cloves

½ teaspoon whole allspice

1 star anise

12 cups water

½ cup brown sugar

1. Wash all the fruit and quarter without coring or peeling, including the orange.

2. Place the fruit and the rest of the ingredients into the Instant Pot inner pot.

3. Secure the lid. Select Slow Cook setting and set for 3 hours.

4. When cook time is up, use a masher to break up the fruit and stir well. Set timer for 1 more hour on Slow Cook setting.

5. Strain through a fine sieve and put into a pitcher. Add sugar according to your taste.

Serving suggestion:

Serve warm.

Kombucha

David Murphy

Makes 1 gallon

3 family-sized black tea bags

¼ teaspoon baking soda

8 cups water, divided

1½ cups granulated sugar

1 SCOBY (look for this at Whole Foods or Amazon)

½ cup vinegar (or 1 cup Kombucha from a previous batch)

1. Place tea bags, baking soda, and 6 cups of water into pot. Place on Manual at high pressure for 4 minutes. Once done, let pressure naturally release.

2. Once done, remove the pot from the machine. Remove tea bags and add sugar. Stir well to dissolve.

3. Pour tea into a sanitized glass 1-gallon container. Add remaining 2 cups of water and vinegar or kombucha from a previous batch. Allow to cool completely. It must be cool to the touch.

4. Add your SCOBY. Cover the top of the container with a coffee filter or piece of cheesecloth and lock in place with a rubber band.

5. Place trivet into your Pot and place glass container onto trivet. Add warm water until it reaches the ⅔ max line. Press Yogurt button with Less Heat. Run the Yogurt cycle for 7 days. Keep out of direct sunlight.

6. Decant and enjoy! Place in the fridge in sanitized bottles and caps, or just use it as you go.

Bubble Tea

Bryan Woolley

Makes 6–8 servings

10 cups water

1 cup brown sugar

2 cups boba tapioca pearls

4 cups brewed black tea

4 tablespoon sweetened condensed milk

Ice, optional

1. Add water, brown sugar, and boba tapioca pearls to Instant Pot. Secure lid and pressure cook on low for 8 minutes. When finished, allow pressure to release naturally.

2. Once pressure is released, remove the lid and stir the tapioca pearls.

3. Carefully spoon ½ cup of boba tapioca pearls into each glass. Fill each glass almost full with brewed tea.

4. Finish off each glass with a large spoonful each of sweetened condensed milk. Stir everything together.

5. If desired, serve over ice.

Index

Conversion Charts

METRIC AND IMPERIAL CONVERSIONS

(These conversions are rounded for convenience)

Ingredient	Cups/ Tablespoons/ Teaspoons	Ounces	Grams/Milliliters
Butter	1 cup/ 16 tablespoons/ 2 sticks	8 ounces	230 grams
Cheese, shredded	1 cup	4 ounces	110 grams
Cream cheese	1 tablespoon	0.5 ounce	14.5 grams
Cornstarch	1 tablespoon	0.3 ounce	8 grams
Flour, all-purpose	1 cup/1 tablespoon	4.5 ounces/0.3 ounce	125 grams/8 grams
Flour, whole wheat	1 cup	4 ounces	120 grams
Fruit, dried	1 cup	4 ounces	120 grams
Fruits or veggies, chopped	1 cup	5 to 7 ounces	145 to 200 grams
Fruits or veggies, pureed	1 cup	8.5 ounces	245 grams
Honey, maple syrup, or corn syrup	1 tablespoon	0.75 ounce	20 grams
Liquids: cream, milk, water, or juice	1 cup	8 fluid ounces	240 milliliters
Oats	1 cup	5.5 ounces	150 grams
Salt	1 teaspoon	0.2 ounce	6 grams
Spices: cinnamon, cloves, ginger, or nutmeg (ground)	1 teaspoon	0.2 ounce	5 milliliters
Sugar, brown, firmly packed	1 cup	7 ounces	200 grams
Sugar, white	1 cup/1 tablespoon	7 ounces/0.5 ounce	200 grams/12.5 grams
Vanilla extract	1 teaspoon	0.2 ounce	4 grams

OVEN TEMPERATURES

Fahrenheit	Celsius	Gas Mark
225°	110°	¼
250°	120°	½
275°	140°	1
300°	150°	2
325°	160°	3
350°	180°	4
375°	190°	5
400°	200°	6
425°	220°	7
450°	230°	8